LITERARY CONJUGATIONS

LITERARY CONJUGATIONS

Edited by Richard T. Gray

This series investigates literary artifacts in their
cultural and historical environments. Through
comparative investigations and case studies across
a wide array of national literatures, it highlights
the interdisciplinary character of literary studies
and explores how literary production extends
into, influences, and refracts multiple domains
of intellectual and cultural life.

W. G. Sebald: A Critical Companion,
edited by J. J. Long and Anne Whitehead

*Speaking Havoc: Social Suffering and South
Asian Narratives*, by Ramu Nagappan

The Linguistics of Lying and Other Essays,
by Harald Weinrich; translated and introduced
by Jane K. Brown and Marshall Brown

The Linguistics of Lying

AND OTHER ESSAYS

HARALD WEINRICH

Translated and Introduced by
Jane K. Brown and Marshall Brown

A Robert B. Heilman Book

UNIVERSITY OF WASHINGTON PRESS

Seattle and London

The Linguistics of Lying and Other Essays *was
published with support from a generous bequest established
by Robert B. Heilman, distinguished scholar and chair
of the University of Washington English Department
from 1948 to 1971. The Heilman Book Fund assists
in the publication of books in the humanities.*

*The publication of this work was supported
by a grant from the Goethe-Institut.*

University of Washington Press
P.O. Box 50096, Seattle, WA 98145
www.washington.edu/uwpress

Library of Congress Cataloging-in-Publication Data
can be found at the back of this book.

The paper used in this publication is acid-free and
recycled from 20 percent post-consumer and at least
50 percent pre-consumer waste. It meets the minimum
requirements of American National Standard for Information Sciences—Permanence of Paper for Printed
Library Materials, ANSI Z39.48‑1984. ♾ ⬤

Contents

Introduction

MARSHALL BROWN

One often hears that the great German philological tradition died out with the generation of Ernst Robert
Curtius, Erich Auerbach, and Leo Spitzer. Harald Weinrich
explodes that myth. While his books have been translated
into many languages, only one has appeared in English,
and that quite recently, and his influence has not crossed
to North America. But let us not mistake our parochial situation for the world. Parochial in two ways: our country
is more monolingual than it should be, and our profes-
sional world is more disciplinary than we imagine, or at
least more limited in its interdisciplinary attentions. While
Weinrich has never denied his roots, his career has reached
out beyond philology, beyond literature, and beyond
Europe to fulfill the vision we ought to have inherited from
the cosmopolitan Curtius, the lonely exile Auerbach, the
linguistically and culturally inquisitive Spitzer. Weinrich's
base of activity, like theirs, lies in old Europe, but the tra-
jectory of his work is greater than that of any of these three,
and it is often expressed in writings like those represented

here—slender in their proportions but astonishingly broad in their compass.

Weinrich is the model post–World War II German intellectual. His life experience is marked by displacement; his mission is to repair the ravages of nationalism; his cause is that of truth in a world where the word had almost lost its meaning. He learned French as an interned adolescent soldier and then proceeded to formal study of the literatures of the erstwhile enemy France, the ally Italy, the bystander Spain. His first book concerned the great adventure novel of all time, Cervantes's *Don Quixote*. The careful reader of its title will do a double if not a triple take. *Das Ingenium Don Quijotes: Ein Beitrag zur literarischen Charakterkunde.* Don Quixote's *intelligence*? A concise, meticulously detailed, deeply learned investigation illuminates the transformations in Cervantes's protagonist (and also in his sidekick, Sancho Panza), leading from madness to . . . to what? That problem is the genii so subtly released by the title. *Ingenium*, wit and talent at once, surprise blended with craft, a concept unformulatable in the German language, is what the *Quixote* offers to those who know how to read it. And how does one learn to read it? The key word here is *Bildung*, a concept as deeply rooted as any in the German tradition. Not just any *Bildung*, above all not the smug, even contemptuous *Bildung* that had been corrupted by the pretensions of the Nazi tyranny, but rather *höfische Bildung*. How to translate that phrase? "Courtly education" gets it all wrong, though nothing in any single language will get so complex a phrase just right. The first sentence of

Weinrich's section on this concept gets to the essential: "The universality of *Bildung* does not mean omniscience." For *Bildung* here is closer to self-cultivation than to any kind of pedagogy or training, and *höfisch* does not mean a regression to monarchical sovereignty. Rather, its principal resonance is courtliness, politeness—in German, *Höflichkeit*. Don Quixote needs to learn above all how to behave, and the others need to learn how to behave toward him. His madness resides in an ideal without a proper vernacular name, the *ingenium* that our modern languages cannot grasp. Indeed, Weinrich's favorite line from Goethe's *Faust*, one of the devil's profound sarcasms, is this: "Man lügt im Deutschen, wenn man höflich ist" (In German, to be polite is to tell a lie). Opening with sections on madness and folly (the latter a philosophical principle, of course), Weinrich, whose precision is always surprising, concludes with a long section on decorum. He reads Cervantes's masterpiece to articulate a "literary science of character," as his subtitle has it—a human science, a humane science—and, as his final line says, to recover "a lost ideal of *Bildung*."

Now, none of this early book is anything more than traditional philology, conducted with loving care ("philology" means, after all, love of the word). It might have been just another critical study, leading to just another successful academic career. Nowhere does it expressly formulate a social vision, a national lesson, a transnational impulse. Politeness could be just another concept, fitted to a book to be admired from a distance. But Weinrich has always pressed forward—beyond language to the truths it can only approximate, beyond abstract ideas to real culture, beyond individual fields of study to the universality of the university, beyond the isolation of the nation to the community of mankind.

Weinrich's first major book, which appeared in 1964, and which has remained his best-known work among literary critics, is *Tempus: Besprochene und erzählte Welt*. Combining linguistics with literary criticism to examine tense use in German, English, and the major Romance languages and literatures, with chapters on Baudelaire, Maupassant, Pirandello, Unamuno, Darío, Echegaray, Hemingway, Boccaccio, Descartes, and Camus, and attentive to nuances of grammar, to genre, to literary and cultural history, to debates in literary and linguistic theory (including a fine-tuned critique of the great linguist Benjamin Whorf, who theorized that languages were untranslatable, nonequivalent world-frames), the book is a subtle, elegant, virtuoso performance. As often in Weinrich's work, the study's central point (here, that tense has no necessary connection with time) seems counterintuitive at the start and utterly commonsensical by the end.

In hindsight, however, *Tempus* appears to be perhaps nothing more than a very grand way station, for literature was in fact leading Weinrich back toward language, and language was leading him toward culture, civilization, and the building (or *Bildung*) of a common humanity. He left his initial position as professor of Romance languages in order to take up a career in historical linguistics. Really, though, his vision was of a cultural linguistics. In his capacity as a linguist, he wrote many dozens of essays, selections of which have been gathered into three substantial collections in German and one in French, that are concerned with the way language has been and should be used. Texts as they are read, language as it is cultivated, in the past and in the present, in high art, in the classroom, in public policy—those are the domains traversed by essays that are at once approachably civilized and daringly exploratory. As a writer and as a person, Weinrich practices the virtues that he has preached from the beginning (and that must have enabled him to triumph over the adversities and evils of his formative years). Unfailingly, he is both polished and polite; everything is orderly; nothing is forced upon the reader, who is both let and left to work with and upon the thoughts so tellingly suggested by writings that are always informed, always formative, always cultivated, always under way, impressive in the highest degree without ever being imposing.

And so, for Weinrich, linguistics both emerged from and led back to the study of culture and cultures, and above all of cultural virtues: memory, forgetting (the topic of the one book, *Lethe*, that has hitherto appeared in English), and politeness, the subject of an iceberg of essays whose brilliant tip shines forth in those that Weinrich has chosen for the second half of the present collection. The culmination of this phase of Weinrich's career, however, is the "text grammars" of French and German. These two massive volumes combine the information about grammatical structures (morphology and syntax) found in conventional grammars with abundant information about usage, both in written texts and in speech situations. The German grammar explains, for instance, how to derive the comparative forms of adjectives, and which adjectives do not have comparative forms, or have them only colloquially, but then it discusses the various uses of comparative forms and surveys other resources the language has for making comparisons, and finally, through page-long commented text extracts, it illustrates the stylistic resources for comparison. The grammars show language as a social tool, not just as a cognitive system. In *Tempus*, Weinrich's closest approach to literary theory, linguistics logically precedes engagement with literary texts; in the grammars, conversely, literary expression functions both practically and programmatically as the best-realized form of linguistic expression. (It is hard to imagine a more perfect realization of "literary conjugations," in both the most crudely literal and the most boldly figurative senses of the phrase.)

From there came Weinrich's third career. He moved to the University of Munich to found the country's first department of German as a foreign language. His approach is neither technical nor sociological, as is characteristic of ESL (English as a second language) specialties in the United States, but rather cultural. The multicultural (or, in the German expression, intercultural) mission is both to acknowledge and enable immigrant groups within the German-speaking countries and also to facilitate commercial and cultural exchange abroad. Weinrich has written abundantly on such diverse topics as the use of memory in language learning and language pedagogy; foreignness and cultural communication; and translation. Retired from his post at Munich, he continued to teach as one of the few foreigners ever hired at France's most prestigious research institution, the Collège de France. The wit and talent, the politeness and Bildung, that he studied in his first book have led him to an ever-expanding devotion to language as the vehicle for mutual understanding.

Weinrich's book-length essay "The Linguistics of Lying" may nevertheless be his most characteristic and all-encompassing expression. It is in part a debate with structural linguistics. It argues that language is inseparable from its concrete usages and usage possibilities, and consequently that it encompasses far more than the formal characteristics that were the accepted province of linguistic study. Textual meaning takes precedence over lexical meaning; or, more simply yet, texts preempt words. Writing in 1965, before all but the very earliest essays of Jacques Derrida, before Paul de Man had popularized the Nietzsche essay that Weinrich cites ("On Truth and Lies in a Nonmoral Sense"), he recognizes figures of speech as vehicles of meaning and thereby points the way toward undoing the skeptical ravages of deconstruction. "The Linguistics of Lying" engages with classical and modern philosophy and theology, with rhetoric, with literary criticism. Weinrich's retrospective comments from the turn of the millennium (appearing in this volume as a preface to the essay) point toward Freud and toward the psychological dimensions of lying. Most daring of all in the body of the original essay are Weinrich's reflections on the Third Reich, which he confesses both as a unique tragedy and yet as a warning example, underestimating neither its particular horrors nor the more general temptations on which it drew. It was bold to write that section in the divided Germany of 1965, with a whole generation of Third Reich participants still active; what keeps it alive today is precisely the modesty of Weinrich's limited, disciplinary perspective, his willingness to state what he sees without claiming a final view. "The Linguistics of Lying" is the challenging, liberating, earnest, and (maybe its highest virtue) friendly expression of a man whose learning and culture know no discernible bounds.

Traduttore, traditore, as the old saying has it; translation betrays. One translates as best one can—and as well as one's language allows. "The Linguistics of Lying" is the title we have chosen for *Linguistik der Lüge,* Harald Weinrich's modest, surprising, sometimes explosive foray between the lines of linguistics, literature, culture, ethics, politics, and history. We think that is what any English speaker would naturally call it. But the German language does not have gerunds, verbal nouns equivalent to our "of —ing" form. Should we have chosen the mechanically literal, if wooden, formula "Linguistics of the Lie"? *Lying* is an action, performed by an agent, with an intention or at least an involvement, an occasion, consequences. *The lie* is the thing itself, disembodied, timeless, abstract. In English, at least, we can make, we are perhaps compelled to make, some such distinction. For a careful English speaker, lying has no linguistics, the lie has no life. German sees things ever so slightly differently. The quiet daring in Weinrich's book, enabled by the grammatical conditions of his language, belongs to the enterprise of bringing the lie to life, of uncovering the actor in the linguistic act, and, conversely, of dissecting the material of which lying is made. There is no merging of matter and spirit, no shirking of the complexities tying us down to the words we have freely uttered, and—as is typical of Weinrich's writing—there are no answers, only questions that open layer upon layer of the human situations beyond the reach of the positive sciences.

Is our translation of his title a lie? Surely there is more to this book than merely an analysis of "lying," that is, of particular behaviors, for there is also a concept, a structure, a history, all of which may be better captured by "the lie" than by "lying." Yet "the lie" is an abstraction, and there is nothing abstract about Weinrich's firmly grounded and precisely circumscribed reflections. There is no way to get the title quite "right," for it operates with unmatched equipoise in the slippery intermediate terrain between unchanging universals and determinate particulars, between truths and facts. That is the domain in which we live our lives, the domain that language opens up to us and condemns us to.

Weinrich's career has been propelled by a quixotic drive toward grammar in an almost medieval sense. He strives for a perfection of language—*Sprachkultur*, another virtually untranslatable formulation—that will embody and illuminate the complexities of experience without rigidifying them. Literature for him is exemplary in two ways, both of which are captured by the term *culture*. First, literature refines the language, polishing it into ever more responsive forms of communication. To that end, literature helps us to become more discriminating, to learn how to discriminate lies from truth, not (as Weinrich reminds us) as we would black from white, but rather as we would sheep from the goats that so often resemble them. And so the book guides us to distinguish words from concepts, lies from metaphors, lexical meanings from contextual significations, pointing toward the angled subtleties we know as metaphor and irony. But if Weinrich is the guide, his own teachers are the great writers—in this case, often great comic writers, such as Lucian of Samosata and Carlo Goldoni and Plato. And if they teach us discrimination and judgment, those are moral as well as intellectual virtues. This is the second exemplary function of literature: as it refines language, so it refines those who use language. And so Weinrich takes his place among the great committed moralists of the age, one whose life has exemplified the virtues that underlie his subtle instruction.

How could the title not be a lie? Human language always falls somewhat short of purity, as does the human condition in general. That is why refinement, *Höflichkeit*, *Bildung* so insistently press in on us. Could the work be presented in the language of the angels, its message would be unsullied. We have given it instead, to the best of our ability, in the language of the English. (Indeed, we have also given English translations of numerous citations and tags that Weinrich gives in Latin and modern Romance languages. The resulting monolingualism falsifies Weinrich's cultured pluralism, but the alternative—translating German citations but not others—would have distorted his work in a different way. We have also gone to considerable trouble to locate and use published English translations wherever possible.) All the tensions of a linguistics of lying, or of the lie, all the utopianism and pathos of *making sense*— that is what this book and this man are about.

This introduction has mentioned Harald Weinrich's principal book publications. His works also include many individual essays and lectures, published separately; several hundred essays published in collections, journals, magazines, and newspapers; numerous edited volumes and translations; and two volumes of poetry. Weinrich's principal books are listed here, in chronological order, with translations of their titles:

1956: *Das Ingenium Don Quijotes: Ein Beitrag zur literarischen Characterkunde* (Don Quixote's Ingenium: A Contribution to the Literary Science of Language)

1964: *Tempus: Besprochene und erzählte Welt* (Tempus: Spoken and Narrated World)

1966: *Linguistik der Lüge* (The Linguistics of Lying)

1971: *Literatur für Leser* (Literature for Readers)

Introduction

1976:   *Sprache in Texten* (Language in Texts)

1982:   *Textgrammatik der französischen Sprache* (Text Grammar of the French Language)

1985:   *Wege der Sprachkultur* (Paths of Language Culture)

1989:   *Conscience linguistique et lectures littéraires* (Language Consciousness and Literary Readings)

1993:   *Textgrammatik der deutschen Sprache* (Text Grammar of the German Language)

1997:   *Lethe: Kunst und Kritik des Vergessens* (*Lethe: The Art and Critique of Forgetting*, trans. Steven Rendall, Cornell University Press, 2004)

2004:   *Knappe Zeit: Kunst und Ökonomie des befristeten Lebens* (Short Time: The Art and Economy of Living with Deadlines)

The Linguistics of Lying

AND OTHER ESSAYS

The Linguistics of Lying

The Linguistics of Lying *was written in 1965. It was composed in response to the first essay competition of the German Academy for Language and Literature: "Can language hide thoughts?" It was published in 1966 and reprinted several times. Then it was out of print for a long time, and now it appears unchanged in its sixth printing. This requires some comment.*

There has been much thinking about linguistics and lying in the thirty-five years that have passed since first publication. An entire library could be filled with recent books and essays on this topic. If I wanted to take account of all this material, I would have to write a new essay. I hesitated to do so, however, since I was uncertain whether that new version could remain an essay at all or would have to become a large book. So I decided to add a preface to the work, as a critical dialogue with the author I was then.

WORD, SENTENCE, TEXT

The "linguistics" tied to lying by alliteration in the title of my essay deserves in retrospect the first consideration. For the science of language, an alternative to the term "linguistics," the sixties were stir-

3

ring times. In Germany, linguistics had just developed from a strictly historical discipline to a structural science of language that undertook to describe how everything in language coheres systematically. This "structuralism," as the new scholarly direction was called, with admiration by its friends and resistance by its opponents, tested its methods by preference on everyday language (this was new) and was even open (this was unheard of) to literary structures.

The scholarly development rapidly jumped ahead—across the Atlantic to "generative grammar," in Central Europe to "text linguistics." That is the historical context for this essay, which was recognized by specialists as a disguised manifesto for text linguistics—called here, because of the topic, "text semantics."

This new linguistics opened a wider field for linguistic analysis by adding the larger dimension "text" to the traditional orientation toward "word" and "sentence." "Word" had been the basis of semantics, the study of lexical meaning; "sentence" had been the basis of syntax, the study of sentences; and generative grammar was about to make the "sentence" the fundamental unit for all of linguistics, including semantics, so that nothing other than direct or indirect sentence forms could be acknowledged as genuine in language.

My position was that text linguistics should do exactly the opposite. The starting point in a given "language game" (in Wittgenstein's sense) should be the oral or written "text in its situation." From there, a text-linguistic analysis descends to examine smaller-scale aspects of language, where various linguistic structures of "text syntax" (not just syntax) and "text semantics" (not just semantics) come into view.

In writing The Linguistics of Lying, I also had the intention, or secondary intention, of testing the capacities of this newly conceived text linguistics on an object that at the time lay far beyond the scope of linguistic and philological methodologies. Until then, lying had been considered a field of activity for philosophers and psychologists, moralists and columnists. For linguists, it was virgin territory. Such an ambitious goal, however, certainly could not be achieved by a single author on the first attempt. In retrospect, I see clearly the limits I faced as spokesman for a young text linguistics. Thus when I reread the piece now, it disturbs me that in an analysis deliberately conceived in terms of text linguistics the word sentence appears so often, if mostly only in the (almost) innocent meaning of "a piece of text." Later, in my text grammars of the French and German languages (1982, 1993), I eliminated the concept of the sentence, since I found it hopelessly illogical with its fixation on the yes/no alternative, and since it is not necessary to a consistent text-linguistic analysis.[1] Had I already possessed, in 1966, more confidence in my own method, many of my observations about lying words and falsified sentences would perhaps have been richer.

LIES OF SHAME, DISGRACE, NEED, AND COMFORT

That understanding the phenomenon of lying required crossing the boundaries even of text linguistics was already clear to me in the sections on metaphor, irony, and poetic fictions, where I availed myself of literary and general cultural modes of understanding, especially those of hermeneutics. But even with a hermeneutics or a poetics, not all strata of lying are accessible, especially when they are hidden in the depths of the soul. Thus I miss in this essay a profound observation like Nietzsche's: "'I did this,' says my memory. 'I cannot have done this,' says my pride, remaining inexorable.

Eventually, my memory yields."[2] Repression gives birth to a pleasant lie with which the moralistic superego is "proudly" hoodwinked into the belief that nothing has happened for which it need take responsibility or atone.

Sigmund Freud showed convincingly in his writings on psychoanalysis how a lie, especially a "life lie" (Henrik Ibsen, The Wild Duck, act 5), repressed into the unconscious, works its havoc secretly, with pathogenic consequences for body and soul. Healing such symptoms requires first curing the psyche of its lies, which can happen only if the process is replayed in the bright light of consciousness and renegotiated to reach the full truth. It is characteristic of Freudian psychoanalysis that it knows no means of curing the underlying illness caused by a repressed lie other than language, which, as narrative, recaptures the hidden sickness and brings it under the control of consciousness. Something like this, and a bit more, could have been in a Freud chapter of my essay if in those days I had had more confidence in interdisciplinary inquiries.[3]

Freud's intellectual advances, however, concern not only the private consciousness but also the public one, and therefore also public and political lying. It is well known that there is a great deal of lying in politics, and that it has increased rather than decreased in recent times. But lying never lay so heavily on an entire country as on Germany under Hitler's dictatorship. I doubt even more now than in 1965 that the corruption of political consciousness caused by this lying can ever be fully described by linguistic means. Public discussion of the day was dominated by the question of whether the German language shared in the disgrace, perhaps even in the guilt, of the crimes that were later identified with terms like Holocaust and Shoah. Under pressure of this discussion, I perhaps paid too little attention to particular voices, especially in literature. At just that moment, the oratorio Die Ermittlung (The Investigation) appeared, in which Peter Weiss condensed the testimony of the first Auschwitz trial into drama. I could have quoted from the words of one of Weiss's witnesses (not even one of the accused) the phrases of lying forgetting: "That's more than I can remember"—"I have no recollection of it"—"I know nothing about that"—"I don't know."[4] Or had this witness before the court perhaps spoken a personal truth because, in the twenty years that at that time had passed since the genocide of the European Jews, even his memory had succumbed to the lie?

Is it possible to avoid lying out of need, for protection, to spare someone? Molière's misanthrope condemns them all, these more or less conventional lies that we ordinary people pay out everyday in small change, now to get out of a minor emergency, now to protect ourselves or someone else temporarily, or to avoid an unpleasant truth with tact. But that upright, honest misanthrope of Molière's is a comic figure whose author has exposed him to ridicule. Real life in society is not such that anyone can "get by" without a little lying and deception—after all, everyone else does it. Only on a desert island—this is the final position of Molière's (tragic?) comedy— can the person who never lies live out his misanthropic caprice. And with this prospect, the audience goes off to supper.[5]

In this context, which also deserved more than a passing remark in my essay, there ought to have been more extensive discussion of politeness. In its old European forms of courtoisie and politesse, it could be called, without scruple, a social virtue were it not that its repertoire of conventions and rituals has opened the door wide to the art of lying. In Schiller's Kabale und Liebe (Love and

Intrigue) a dialogue begins: "'I hope I do not interrupt your lady-ship?' 'Not at all, baron, not in the least'" (act 2, scene 3).[6] They are deadly enemies, Major Ferdinand von Walter and Lady Milford, yet they begin this conversation about their true relationship to one another with these conventional lies. Our classical literature lives from such forms of courteous-courtly gallantry, which, seen in the light (but in what light?), are at once delicate and enormous lies. Yet they belong, or belonged for centuries, so obviously to the elegant illusoriness of aristocratic, bourgeois, and diplomatic conduct that they can no longer be judged with such sharp-edged concepts as truth and lie. Here, Karl Kraus's discussion of "lying society" might have helped us.[7] But in Jurek Becker's novel Jakob der Lügner (Jacob the Liar), which appeared only in 1969, that would no longer have been sufficient.[8] In this profound novel from out of the despair of the Warsaw Ghetto, the Jew Jakob is a frivolously daring liar who daily invents new radio bulletins for his companions about the imminent liberation, and in this fashion keeps a tiny ray of hope alive for them until the bitter end of the illusion. The number of suicides in the ghetto drops for a while; the number of murders at the end does not.

Who is actually lying in this "novel," when Jakob the liar lies?

HARALD WEINRICH

Paris, 2000

"MAGNA QUAESTIO EST DE MENDACIO . . ."

Lying exists in the world. It is in and around us. It cannot be overlooked. "Omnis homo mendax," say the Psalms (115:11).[9] We might translate: man is a being capable of lying. This definition has the same validity as those that call man a being who can think, speak, or laugh. It may well be a misanthropic definition, but it is irrefutable. Molière's misanthrope derives from it the right to hate all of humanity.

Linguistics cannot rid the world of lying, nor can it prevent "the banners of lying" (Goethe, *Faust*, line 10405) from being so frequently unfurled. To be sure, people lie—mostly—by means of language; they tell lies and they *speak* with forked tongues. But it is highly questionable whether language helps them lie. If it does, then linguistics probably cannot escape the "great problem of lying" (Augustine). If, however, language does not further lying, or even resists it, linguistics can nevertheless describe what happens in language when truth is distorted into lie. Certainly, lying is of concern to linguistics.

Augustine, the first to make lying the object of philosophical and theological reflection, was also the first to recognize its linguistic aspect. He points out that language is not given to men for mutual deceit, but for the exchange of ideas. Anyone who uses language to deceive, therefore, misuses it, and that is sin.[10] Thomas Aquinas and Bonaventure pursue these ideas. Words in language are signs of the spirit; it goes against their nature and against the spirit to use them in service of lying.[11] Language should reveal thought, not hide it. At stake is the signifying function of language, its most elementary, consequently most fundamental, achievement. Lying perverts it.

Humans are so constructed, however, that they use the signs of language simultaneously for good and evil. So say the moralists. A hexameter of Dionysius Cato reads: "Sermo hominum mores et celat et indicat idem" ("Men's practice, words may hide as well as tell"; language simultaneously hides and reveals human morals).[12] His skeptical doctrine attracted its followers. Voltaire writes a dialogue between a cock and a hen, and puts in the beaks of his high-flying orators this harsh judgment of the human race: "They only apply their minds to excuse their injustices; they only use words to cover up their thoughts."[13] If you don't believe the cock, perhaps Talleyrand will persuade you. He is traditionally supposed to have remarked, in conversation with the Spanish ambassador Izquierdo in 1807, "Speech was given to man to hide his thoughts."[14] His remark has become proverbial. It is also ascribed to Fouché or to Metternich. This means, even if not everyone uses language to conceal thoughts, that among politicians and diplomats lying is part of the profession. It is an art. Hermann Kesten takes this idea up and unfolds it like a fan: "People automatically assume there are entire professions that force their members to lie, for example, theologians, politicians, whores, diplomats, poets, journalists, lawyers, artists, actors, forgers, stockbrokers, food industrialists, judges, doctors, gigolos, generals, cooks, wine merchants."[15] Is this a poet speaking?

Time and again, voices are raised to blame language when it is misused for lying. Shakespeare's *Henry V* says—in French, in English, and in a mixture—"O bon dieu! Les langues des hommes sont pleines de tromperies . . . the tongues of men are full of deceits . . . de tongues of de

mans is be full of deceits" (act 5, scene 2, lines 115–20).
Perhaps, indeed, some languages more than others. In
Goethe's *Wilhelm Meister's Apprenticeship*, the company discusses at one point the pros and cons of French theater.
They notice that Aurelie remains withdrawn from the discussion of this theme. Gentle pressure elicits her reason:
she hates the French language. Her faithless lover has
ruined it for her. For as long as he was true to her, he wrote
his letters in German, "and what genuine, powerful, cor-
dial German!" But when he withdrew his love, he switched
to French, which he had previously used only in jest. Aurelie
understood the change only too well. "It is the language of
reservations, equivocations, and lies: it is a *perfidious* language. . . . French is exactly the language of the world—
worthy to become the universal language, that all may have
it in their power to cheat and cozen and betray each other!"[16]
If Aurelie is right in her "peevish lamentations," then
German would be the language of truth, French that of lies.

These are, of course, only anecdotes and not meant otherwise by Shakespeare and Goethe. But it could be the case
that language in general, as Wittgenstein once speculated, is not the guise of thought but its disguise.[17] Such
doubts are often encountered. When scholars in all disciplines gathered several years ago to examine the phenomenon of lying, the linguist Friedrich Kainz was invited
to present a paper on manifestations of lying in speech.[18]
Following Augustine, Kainz initially identifies all lies as
speech acts, and therefore part of language. He then exam-
ines language for prevarication and finds so much that the

reader must shake in his boots. Just as one can say that language thinks and writes for us, so, according to Friedrich Kainz, one can say with equal justice that it lies for us. He coins for this the expression "the seduction of language." He asserts that our thinking follows linguistic paths, and that therefore the lies inherent in language also force our thought into lying. But, on closer examination, linguistic lies include the majority of rhetorical figures, such as euphemisms, hyperbole, ellipses, amphibole, the forms and formulas of politeness, emphasis, irony, verbal taboos, anthropomorphisms, etc. Only a narrow lane indeed is left for truth. That, as one might expect, is the simple declarative statement logicians love.

What a sad critique—it has stripped language of all its blossoms and leaves and has only a spindly stem left in its hand! Augustine was a better linguist than that, for he had already addressed this question. In his work *Against Lying*, Augustine confronts the difficulty of justifying Jacob's nasty deception of Isaac to steal the right of the firstborn (Genesis, chapter 27) and of reconciling it with his categorical condemnation of lying. His solution: it "is not a lie but a mystery." The biblical event is a mystery that must be understood allegorically. Jacob covers his hand with a goatskin, not to deceive his father but as the type of the expected savior, who takes the sins of others upon himself. To call it a lie would force us to consider all other forms of nonliteral language, all tropes, images, and metaphors, as lies. And that would be "a deplorable consequence," that is to say, arrant nonsense.[19]

It is thus inadequate, Augustine continues, to define lying as saying something other than what one knows or means. With such a definition it is not possible to distinguish serious, evil lies from the playful forms ("ioci") of cultivated discourse, for these latter can be taken as allegories, that is to say, "speaking the other." Moral consciousness tells us something different. There is lying only when "speaking the other" is accompanied by a conscious intention to deceive. Hence Augustine's famous definition of lying: "A lie is any pronouncement whatsoever accompanied by a desire to deceive."[20] The scholastics adopted this definition and passed it on to European philosophy. Discussions in moral philosophy henceforth address only the limiting cases of the definition of lying. Are lies permitted in emergencies? Is there any such thing as "pious deceit"? Do the means justify the end? Thus it is always a question of whether the (evil) intention to deceive, which has been considered the essence of lying since Augustine, can be balanced by any good intention somehow connected to the lie. I will leave the decision to moral philosophers; in this case, the linguists have no vote.

The question, however, is whether under Augustine's definition linguists have any vote at all on the *magna quaestio* of lying. Lying seems to withdraw from the linguists' area of competence. Whether a statement is true or false must be assessed according to the facts. And whether or not there is an intention to deceive is decided within the soul and is thus accessible, if at all, only to psychological consideration. It makes sense that linguists have not exactly seen in Augustine's definition of lying an invitation to engage with this phenomenon. Apart from the genial insights of occasional outsiders, therefore, lying does not appear in grammars and other books on language. The reflections in this essay are an attempt to explore lying as a linguistic topic and, in addition, to gain from lying, however much it should be condemned, the benefit of otherwise unavailable information about language. It can perhaps yield some information on whether language can hide thoughts, and how that takes place. It will be necessary, in the process, to remind ourselves of a few basic facts of linguistics. Hence we shall make a brief detour from the phenomenon in order to confront it more fully armed.

WORD AND TEXT

Are lies told with words? Are lies told with sentences? Is lying a phenomenon of semantics or of syntax? We'll try semantics first, starting by saying what meaning actually is.

If language is a system of signs, then one might imagine the following process. Here is a speaker, and here is a listener. Let's assume linguistic communication being established between the two by the speaker transmitting to the listener the linguistic sign *fire.* Let's assume further that there is no context. Similarly, no particular situation in real life is associated with this communication. I hasten to say that the communication just described is entirely fictive and has only the value of a model. We do not normally speak in separate words but in sentences and texts, and our speech is embedded in a situation. But I also hasten to say that in the scant century of its existence as a science, semantics has always worked with this fiction and concerned itself almost exclusively with single words. We shall do the same, but only for a moment.

The listener who has received the verbal sign *fire* according to the above model of communication can't do much with it. Its informational content is minimal. Still, he does know something. From among the very large number of words conceivable in this process of communication, one has been selected, and as a result many things have already become unlikely topics of conversation. But the listener still has no idea what kind of fire is in question. It could be on a stove or in straw, a conflagration or a candle flame, blazing or flickering, real or imagined. The listener doesn't even know if fire is the real topic. It could be fiery wine, the fire of love, or a shot from a gun. The listener has the meaning of the word *fire*, but in its range (its "extension") it is broad. The dictionary entry for *fire*, which is fairly long, reflects graphically the breadth of the word's lexical meaning.

First principle of semantics: every lexical meaning is *broad*.

Is clear communication even possible if as a matter of principle every lexical meaning is broad? The speaker may perhaps want to talk about a conflagration, and the listener thinks about a stove burner or something entirely different. More precisely, he still has no idea what to be thinking about. His comprehension remains suspended in a state of expectation for further information. Without it, and this was the assumption of our model, the (broad) lexical meaning of the verbal sign *fire* remains vague for the listener, in terms of its content (its "intension").

Second principle of semantics: every lexical meaning is *vague*.

Even so, it is not totally useless for the speaker to entrust the verbal sign *fire* to the air waves, as long as he thereby reaches hearers in his language community. For *fire* has the same (broad, vague) lexical meaning to all members of the same language community. The lexical meaning of the word doesn't give them much, but this "not much" is held in common by a large group. Hence the large group shares identical expectations about what information might be forthcoming. That makes lexical meaning a social formation.

Third principle of semantics: every lexical meaning is *social*.

Suppose now, for a moment, that we as nonparticipating observers have figured out from some indication or other that the speaker means a conflagration he witnessed. This conflagration can be described in all its specificity as a unique occurrence. The listener, who has access only to the word *fire* and its lexical meaning, learns practically nothing of all these details. With the (broad, vague, social) lexical meaning he receives only scanty data, which could be crudely characterized with the qualities "hot," "burning." He learns no other details of this particular fire. The verbal sign *fire* establishes a horizon of relevance for the characteristics of this fire; some characteristics (very few) are assumed to be relevant, and the rest (as many as one likes) are considered irrelevant and are not included in the lexical meaning of the word. The sum total of characteristics taken to be relevant to an object by a language community is what we call "lexical meaning." This procedure of sorting the qualities of an object in terms of relevance is a process of abstraction. Lexical meaning established in this fashion is an abstraction. This applies to all lexical meanings, not just to those of words normally considered abstract, like *truth* or *democracy.*

Fourth principle of semantics: every lexical meaning is *abstract.*

Of course, the four principles of semantics are related, indeed are really four aspects of the same thing. Since the lexical meanings of words are broad, they can only be vague. (The scope and the content of lexical meanings are inversely proportional.) But because lexical meanings are vague, they can be used in a social group. So lexical meaning is simultaneously poor and rich. What poverty of information in the word *flower*, what a wealth of qualities in each individual flower! But conversely as well: what limitation in the individual object, what power of evocation in a word! Mallarmé knew this: "When I say: 'a flower!' then from that forgetfulness to which my voice consigns all floral form, something different from the usual calyces arises, something all music, essence, and softness: the flower which is absent from all bouquets."[21] The flower as word that cannot be found in any bouquet is superior to every real flower. It contains more mystery.

Yet there is a disconcerting word in Mallarmé's declaration—the word *idée* (here rendered as "essence"). It is a warning to every semanticist that he has come into the vicinity of Plato's doctrine of ideas. Lexical meanings as broad, vague, social, and abstract constructs resemble Plato's ideas to a worrisome degree, naturally with the difference that each language community must be imagined with its own realm of ideas or lexical meanings, Nietzsche's "conceptual heaven" or Weisgerber's "intellectual mediary world" ("geistige Zwischenwelt").[22] But neither Plato nor semantics is particularly well served by that. Should we therefore, in order to escape the (unfortunately) compromised proximity to Plato, follow the skeptical tendency of modern semantics and language philosophy and renounce any concept of meaning? Paul Valéry, who thought a lot about semantic questions in the wake of Mallarmé, considers this possibility in his notebooks around 1900–1901: "The meaning of a word exists only in each particular usage."[23] Better known is Ludwig Wittgenstein's remark in his *Philosophical Investigations* (I cite the entire sentence because the important reservation is usually overlooked): "For a *large* class of cases—though not for all—in which we employ the word 'meaning' it can be defined thus: the meaning of a word is its use in the language."[24]

We shall neither agree with Valéry and Wittgenstein nor leave semantics stranded in the vicinity of the Platonic doctrine of ideas. Instead we shall construct a synthesis of this thesis and antithesis and develop these reflections further into a *dialectical semantics*. It is high time to put aside the model we began by postulating. Let us free the word from its isolation, set it in the framework of its context, and set both in a real-life situation. This is how we normally encounter words. The dictionary is the exception, not the rule. And a good dictionary, even if it can't characterize the whole situation, gives words at least the modest context of examples in sentences.

Words belong, therefore, in sentences, texts, and situations. These must be taken into account in order for us to understand what a word is and how it relates to its lexical meaning; otherwise we are in constant confusion. The four principles of semantics just established characterize only half of semantics. They apply only to the scarcely more than fictive model of communication by isolated words, without context and situation. They don't apply to words in general, and they especially don't apply to words as we normally use them, namely, in a text (spoken or written). The semantics of words in a text is completely different from the semantics of isolated individual words, and word semantics must be supplemented by text semantics. The old semantics was largely a semantics of words; it banished everything that crossed the boundary from word to sentence into syntax. But syntax is something entirely different. It begins only on the far side of text semantics.

Text semantics has corollaries to the four principles named above, and they are just as important as the original principles. Any real-life situation can illustrate them. There the speaker is in a dilemma. He wants to tell the listener about a particular, unique fire, which has become important for him and worthy of being reported, but he has at his disposal only words, with their broad, vague, social, and abstract lexical meanings. All other possible meanings of the word *fire* are of no interest to him; that's not what he means. He has, therefore, while he makes use of a *lexical meaning* [*Bedeutung*], a *textual meaning* [*Meinung*] that is not identical to it. This textual meaning is not broad; rather, it is narrowly circumscribed. It refers to this single object, this conflagration he wants to report. Nor is the textual meaning vague; rather, it is very precise. Furthermore, it isn't social but individual—what he personally wants to say here and now. And it is, finally, not abstract but concrete. None of the many qualities of this conflagration is suppressed in the speaker's textual meaning for the sake of some particular point of view. Thus we can summarize the four corollaries of semantics: every textual meaning is narrow, precise, individual, and concrete. These four corollaries obviously belong together and depend on one another, just as the four principles of semantics do.

Lexical and textual meaning are the two fundamental concepts of semantics. Everything that can be said about semantics depends on one or the other of these poles, and only what depends on both deserves the name *semantics*. Our presentation thus far began from the pole of lexical meaning and from there identified that of textual meaning. A presentation oriented toward language development would proceed in the reverse direction. Language is learned through sentences and texts. In the beginning are textual meanings, at first very few, then, with increasing linguistic experience, many, all derived from heard and remembered sentences. But there are not only textual meanings; from them lexical meaning—actually a hypothetical construct—is assembled. With this, the second semantic pole has been reached, and the word is learned. Now it can be used independently. The hypothetical lexical meaning is then constantly adjusted through usage in one's own sentences. As speakers of a language, we engage daily in the play of hypothesis formation and verification or falsification, the same play to which science has committed itself. In terms of its structure, language is a pre-scientific science.[25]

I return to the dilemma of the speaker with an intention (or textual meaning, in the sense defined above) who must make use of words with their lexical meanings. Voltaire expresses the dilemma in this fashion. You have at your disposal, he writes in his *Philosophical Dictionary*, the words *love* and *hate*. But there are thousands of kinds of love and hate in real life. How can one possibly do justice to all the nuances! Voltaire draws a pessimistic conclusion: all languages are imperfect, as are all human beings. Nathalie Sarraute has the same scruples. She—or, to be more exact, the narrator of the novel *Portrait of a Man Unknown*—starts to discuss Prince Bolkonski's great love in Tolstoi's *War and Peace* and immediately despairs of communicating the prince's feelings by means of the word *love*: "As always, it is impossible to escape these big words that bowl us right over."[26]

No, that is not semantics. Of course, there is nothing more multiform than love; everyone knows that. And, of course, there is only the one word *love* (at least in French it has a plural). But that is no reason to blame languages for imperfection. For in the face of the thousands of kinds of love, there is not only the one word *love* but also thousands of sentences about love. And even if the lexical meaning of the word *love* is always the same, its textual meaning in each sentence is different. The sentence is the bridge between lexical meaning and textual meaning. The sentence, together with its context and surrounding situation, limits the (broad, vague, social, abstract) lexical meaning to the (narrow, precise, individual, concrete) textual meaning. A word heard in isolation sets the mind wandering through the whole circuit of meanings. If the word is heard in a text, that is no longer possible. The context fixes—that is, it fixes the meaning. The words of the text limit and restrict one another, and the more complete the text is, the more effectively they do this. Here, from one of the Grimms' fairy tales, is an example of a context for the word *fire*: "Now, for the first time, the soldier took a good look around hell. There were kettles all about, and they were boiling and bubbling with tremendous fires under each one of them."[27] Our word is part of a sentence, and the context of the other words reduces its meaning to the intention of the fairy tale. We see how easily this takes place. The determinant "around hell" excludes all fires that are not the fires of hell; the adjective "tremendous" excludes all hell fires that aren't tremendous, and in the same way the remaining words in the sentence all contribute to specifying the meaning of the word *fires* as exactly as possible.

What remains is narrow, precise, individual, and concrete: the textual meaning of the Brothers Grimm at this unique point in the text "The Devil's Sooty Brother." No matter that the precision of the language goes no further, and that we know no more details about the fire. The precision has evidently achieved the degree appropriate to the imaginations of children and adults reading fairy tales. We mustn't forget that the text of the entire tale continues to add to the determination.

It is clear, in any case, how the context shapes a word's textual meaning from its lexical meaning. In effect, it cuts away pieces of the broad meaning that cannot be reconciled with the neighboring meanings in the sentence. After all the cuts have been made, what remains is the textual meaning. We designate the process *determination* and refer to Spinoza's old theorem, "Limitation is negation."[28] Of course, all the neighboring words are determined as well. "Kettles" determines "fires," and "fires" determines "kettles." No special logical constructs are necessary. Simply the fact that two words stand next to one another causes them to mutually determine one another. Even so, in most sentences we also use function words (prepositions, conjunctions, etc.) for the purposes of determination. Thus a text is more than a sequence of words, and (unlike dictionaries) it communicates more than a mass of lexical meanings. It adds to the sum of the words the determination; or, more precisely, from the sum of the lexical meanings it subtracts something—most of it—and thereby establishes *sense*. The sense is the result deriving from the plus of the lexical meanings and the minus of the determinations.

As a consequence, the old argument about whether word or text (sentence) comes first is rendered moot. What is present first and always is *the word in the text*. And if there ever is a primary interpretation of the world through the words of individual languages, then it is always already superseded in texts. We are not the slaves of words, because we are the masters of texts.

The old complaint that languages are basically untranslatable becomes equally moot. German *Gemüt*, like French *esprit* and American *business*, are all supposed to be elusive. Dilettantish arguments of this sort are as worthless as they are annoying. The words *Feuer*, *rue*, *car* aren't translatable either. No word is translatable. But we don't ever have to translate words. We translate sentences and texts. It doesn't matter that the lexical meanings of words don't usually correspond exactly from one language to another. The issue in the text is really the textual meanings, and we can handle these adequately—just by making the context correspond. In principle, therefore, texts are translatable. So are translations lies? The following rule should serve: translated words always lie, but translated texts lie only when they are badly translated.

WORD AND CONCEPT

Criticism of language is just as old as reflection about language. It shows that language always necessarily lags behind thought. After all, thought aims for a single truth, but words belong to the many separate languages, and lead us at best to a German, English, French truth, never to the truth. "Rem tene, verba sequentur," as Cato the Elder advised (Hold fast to the thing, and the words will follow),[29] and in his wake there have been many who advised paying more attention to things than to words. Even the linguistics of our time has set about taking his advice punctiliously to heart. "Words and things" is the formula for a linguistic methodology that has seemed especially appropriate for describing dialects. The formula should be understood as "Fewer words, more things." The dialect researcher had more confidence in the object *plow* than in the various words that designate it in particular dialects. This led to a separate branch of linguistics called *onomastics* (the study of naming). Its methodological principle: study words from things. The things come first, the words second. In onomastics, linguistics lost its way.

But onomastics only retraced, in the field of concrete objects, what had long been evident in the realm of the mind, namely, that linguistics suffers from an inferiority complex in relation to the other human and natural sciences, especially logic and mathematics. It was not thought proper to pay more attention to words than to ideas, and so it was necessary to invoke the logos and to hide the offensive particularity of words behind their more respectable generality. What are words, after all? Nietzsche wrote, "The various languages placed side by side show that with words it is never a question of truth, never a question of adequate expression; otherwise there would not be so many languages."[30] And what are languages, after all? Natural languages, they are called, and they are natural in the same sense that natural sons or daughters are natural. They can just as well be called illegitimate. To escape the lying of natural languages, it is necessary to give them up and construct artificial ones. That's what logic does, and mathematics also. Condillac states his expectations clearly: "Algebra is a well-structured language, in fact the only one; nothing in it seems arbitrary."[31] Use of an artificial language has become so obvious in logic and mathematics that eyebrows are raised when a popularizing logician or mathematician eschews it.

Behind all this stands a conviction, widespread among scholars and scientists, that words are but the inadequate clothing of thoughts, antiquated national garb. It would be better to get rid of them; they only get in the way. Hold fast to the thing, and the words will follow: this maxim applies even when the thing is a concept. If linguistics occasionally proclaims it high time for conceptual dictionaries that arrange words according to predetermined categories in a general system of concepts, that is simply the methodological consequence of the inveterate insecurity of linguistics.

Natural languages really have no reason to be ashamed

of their nature. They contain just as much truth as the language of logic and mathematics. That is immediately clear when languages are measured by their own standards, and not by standards taken from the technical language of other disciplines. Words do not distort thoughts, for the simple reason that we do not speak in isolated words, but in sentences and texts. So if words are to be compared to concepts, then they must be compared under appropriate conditions, that is to say, in texts. In that case, the mystique of concepts goes up in smoke.

What are concepts, actually? Concepts are above all—nothing special. We encounter them every day and we use them every day. If you're sick, you encounter the concept *fever*; if you're in court, you deal with the concept *oath*; and if you're a chemist, you work with the concept *catalyst*. Concepts are at home primarily in the language of the sciences. It is irrelevant, it is often claimed, that these three concepts happen to be identified by the three English words *fever*, *oath*, *catalyst*; they could equally well be named with the German words *Fieber*, *Eid*, *Katalysator* or with the French words *fièvre*, *serment*, *catalyseur*. Just as dialect scholars point to a plow and elicit various words, scientists can point to their concepts and elicit their names in the different languages. The very fact that there are different names for any given concept is considered an evil and a source of possible misunderstandings. And not just that but, in principle, an actual source of scientific error. Thus the scholarly world has an interest in normalizing, as much as possible, the names of its concepts in the various languages. It does so by elevating words from Greek or Latin into the ranks of neutral norms and then recommending them to the individual languages for naming disciplinary concepts. That is why, for example, the words *fever, Fieber, fièvre* and the words *catalyst, Katalysator, catalyseur* are so similar in their sound structures. Of course, it would be better, the claims continue, if the names were identical, just as the sign *x* is the same everywhere in the language of mathematics. But languages have been different ever since Babel, and we'll just have to manage with the inadequacy of natural languages as a *conditio humana*. Normalizing committees are at work everywhere to minimize their troublesome effects.

However often they are repeated, such arguments do not invalidate the truth of language. None of it is any reason to see anything extraordinary in scientific concepts, which the words of particular languages strive after as a forever unattainable idol. There are no concepts stored outside individual languages. Rather, concepts are nothing other than words, and that always means words in a particular language. But they are words whose lexical meanings are treated specially. How that takes place will now be examined more closely. Let us take as an example the word and concept *fever*.

This word in the English language is, like all words, not designed to be used alone. It is normally at home in texts. That might be a sentence having to do with a "feverish search." In this text, as in all texts, the lexical meaning of the word *fever* is determined, by the context, toward a particular textual meaning. A doctor will say, of course, "What does that have to do with fever! That isn't the medical concept *fever* the way it is used at a patient's bedside." But if you ask the doctor what characterizes the concept *fever* so that a feverish search cannot ever be included, then he will say, "We use the term *fever* when and only when the body temperature rises above 98.6°Fahrenheit." This answer will satisfy the semanticist. It confirms for him what he wants to see confirmed for all words, namely, that they normally occur in sentences. Definitions are sentences, too. Now, since the concepts of the sciences are constructed by means of definitions, and only by means of definitions, what the semanticist hears above all from this is that concepts originate by means of sentences, and only by means of sentences. Concepts belong, therefore, to the realm of text semantics, not word semantics. The definition is the context for the concept. Concepts do not have the semantic status of isolated words but that of words in texts.

Words in texts no longer have (broad, vague, social, abstract) lexical meaning but (narrow, precise, individual, concrete) textual meaning. This is true for concepts as well. But with an essential condition that follows from the nature of definition. There are many forms of definition— that will not occupy us here.[32] But in semantic terms, what all definitions have in common is that they involve relatively short texts. Usually it is a sentence like, for example, "Fever is a body temperature above 98.6° Fahrenheit." This one sentence alone is pertinent to the status of the

English word *fever* as a concept of medical science. For words in everyday language, by contrast, the entire context is important, and the situation as well. One wants to express oneself clearly and communicate to one's interlocutor exactly what he needs to know here and now. All I have to do is place the word *fire* in a conversation and set the conversation in an unambiguous situation; with context and situation, I will have achieved a determination of the lexical meaning of *fire* into a textual meaning with maximum precision. It is, we may imagine, the conflagration the hearer sees in that very moment.

The precision of a word fully determined by context and situation far exceeds that of any concept, even the most exact scientific one. Concepts are words that are only imperfectly determined. Some determination of the word's lexical meaning in the direction of textual meaning has taken place, but only to a limited extent. The determining context is relatively small, and a determining situation is "by definition" excluded. Accordingly, a concept is a word that remains suspended between the poles of lexical meaning and textual meaning. Its degree of conceptualization is neither completely specific nor completely unspecific, but it has exactly that grade of specificity that is appropriate for scientific usage.

Between the poles of lexical meaning and textual meaning there is actually a *sliding scale* that runs from broad to narrow, vague to precise, social to individual, abstract to concrete. Context and situation are the regulators that allow us to set whatever value we like on this scale. Everyday speech, which normally involves a substantial component of situational determinants, usually hovers at the pole of textual meaning or very close to it. Personal names, too, are, as words, very close to the pole of textual meaning and have therefore strong determining power. Words in a book title, which lack situational determinants and often have minimal or no context, lie, by contrast, at or very near the pole of lexical meaning. (Reading the book supplies the missing contextual determination and releases the tension of the title.) Concepts, then, according to their type and the quality of their definition, sit somewhere in the middle of the semantic scale, normally closer to lexical meaning than to textual meaning. After all, they are supposed not only to cover individual, concrete, precise, narrow cases but also to be applicable to the entire realm of the sciences. Thus a sick child who tells the doctor examining her, "I have a really bad fever," gives the word, through the context and the situation, a more precise textual meaning than the concept *fever* ever has in a scientific treatise and indeed ever can have if it is to remain a general, scientific term. Applied to the case of our sick child, the concept might well be further determined, perhaps by the text that tells the history of the illness, and thereby brought closer to the pole of textual meaning; but for the conceptual nature of the word *fever*, that is irrelevant.

Concepts do not exist *before* language, in some unimaginable kind of speech-free thought, but *in* language; more precisely, in a particular language; even more precisely, *in sentences* of this language. They are more exact than isolated words, less exact—normally—than everyday words in texts and situations. Their intermediate precision has served the sciences well.

But don't concepts have an exchange value that extends across the borders of individual languages? How does that fit with their being words in particular languages? It works beautifully, so long as we don't lose the text for the words. The German word *Fieber* has one lexical meaning. The English word *fever* has a different one, and the French word *fièvre* yet another. For scientific communication, which is in principle supranational, it would be a terrible difficulty if scientists had to communicate in isolated words. But they communicate in sentences, and with the aid of their contexts it is possible, fortunately, to set the different lexical meanings of the words *Fieber, fever, fièvre* on a normalized semantic scale so that the set value is identical in all the languages. This takes place by means of definition, which can be understood semantically as a normed and normalizing context for a word. Let the German, English, and French words be as different as they like: as concepts—that is, partially determined by the brief context of a definition—they are identical. They don't stop being words in their own languages, but they are tied to particular contexts and to that extent have the same conceptual value. That's what I meant by saying at the beginning that concepts are nothing special. They come no closer to truth than other words do. They don't reveal thoughts better than other words do. Their sole advantage over other words is their suitability for use in the international discussion of the sciences.

But they are also no worse. Spengler's assertion, "Concepts kill Being,"[33] is just as false as the complementary assertion, "Words disguise thinking."

CAN WORDS LIE?

"Your husband is dead, and sends his greeting."[34] This message that Goethe's Mephistopheles delivers to Frau Marthe Schwerdtlein is a lie. Mephisto has no idea whether or not Herr Schwerdtlein is dead, and in any case he has no regards from him. Most lies are of this sort. They are sentences. There is no doubt that sentences can lie.

But can words also lie? Here, of course, I don't mean the conceivable situation in which Mephisto, for example, answers a question or a questioning glance from Frau Marthe with "Dead." In such a situation, determined by the context of the dialogue, the lexical meaning of the word *dead* is restricted, with full clarity. There can't be any doubt that only one of the many possible meanings of the word *dead* is operative here, namely, the one that applies to the decease of the faraway Herr Schwerdtlein. The lexical meaning is just as determined into textual meaning as in the sentence that Goethe actually wrote as a line in *Faust.*

What is really meant is the question of whether words can lie all by themselves, of whether a lie can inhere in the lexical meaning of a word itself. Such is often claimed. Here are three examples. Among the five difficulties in writing the truth described by Bertolt Brecht in 1934 "for distribution in Hitler's Germany" is the difficulty that arises from the "rotting mystique" of words. There stands the unforgettable sentence, "In our time anyone who says *population* in place of *people* or *race*, and *privately owned land* in place of *soil*, is by that simple act withdrawing his support from a great many lies."[35] The examples are naturally replaceable, given that we no longer live in Brecht's time. In a questionnaire based on Brecht, Stefan Andres elaborates—and, to be sure, also simplifies—Brecht's notion: "Indeed, even the word *truth* travels these days under a quarantine flag, as do freedom, justice, tolerance, loyalty, honor, and many others; all these concepts are completely infected—with ideology, pragmatism, and fallacious justifications of all sorts."[36] Answering the same questionnaire, Reinhard Baumgart nurses similar worries about the word *truth*. "The word itself, I fear, has already lost its balance and tends to the opposite of what it ought to mean: to lie."[37] In Eugen Rosenstock-Huessy we find the formula we would expect in this connection. He accuses the spirit of the age of fathering lies and oppressing us with its "mendacious slogans."[38] Never did slogans run so rampant in Germany as during the Hitler regime. Did the German language become thereby a language of lies? Have its words been dehumanized? Or were they only collaborators? Or were they perhaps not affected at all?

Doubtless, words that have been used in great measure for lying become untruthful. Just try using a word like *Weltanschauung* [worldview], *Lebensraum* [living space], *Endlösung* [final solution]: even the very tongue resists and spits it out. Anyone who uses it regardless is either a liar or the victim of a lie. Lies ruin more than style; they ruin language. Nor is there any therapy for ruined words; they must be expelled from the language. The sooner and more thoroughly that happens, the better for our language.

But how is it actually possible for words to lie? Do the words *table*, *fire*, and *stone* also lie? It is certainly the case that the tyrants who lied to us year after year also used these words. This question, too, cannot be addressed without a dependable theory of semantics.[39] Because not every word can lie. It is also not the case, as a superficial examination might suggest, that abstract words can perhaps lie but not concrete ones. The semantic boundary between words that can lie and those that cannot runs elsewhere.

Let us examine two German words that have been used for a great deal of lying. I mean the word *Blut* [blood] and the word *Boden* [soil]. Both words can still be used today, as always, with no problem. People don't use them for lying and are not lied to by them. But it is impossible for any German ever again to use them together. *Blut und Boden* can be used only for lying, as the combination always was. Is that perhaps the fault of the tiny word *und* (and)? No, this word is completely innocent. It is because in juxtaposition the two words *Blut* and *Boden* contextualize one another. The context *und Boden* determines the lexical meaning of the word *Blut* into the Nazi textual meaning; and, similarly, the lexical meaning of the word *Boden* is determined in the Nazi sense by the context *Blut und*. The speaker is no longer at the pole of lexical meaning but has used context to select a value on the semantic scale between the poles of lexical meaning and textual meaning—a value about at the point where concepts are located.

This is generally true. Words thought of without contextual determination cannot lie. But all it takes is a little context, like a connection with *and*, for words to lie. Concepts are such that they come into being only through context. Without definition there is no concept. And they survive only as long as this context, this definition, is known. It doesn't matter if the defining context is not named every time the concept is mentioned. That is often unnecessary, especially when the concept is applied in the framework of acknowledged scientific expressions. This frame establishes as a rule of the game that the definitions are known and acknowledged. Then they don't have to be stated every time; the determination of the lexical meaning—that is, its limitation to the value of the concept—continues.

Therefore, concepts can lie even when they stand alone. For they only seem to stand alone. An unspoken context stands behind them: the definition. Lying words are almost without exception lying concepts. They belong to a system of concepts and have a place in an ideology. They become untruthful when the ideology and its doctrines are untruthful.

Words can often be convicted of lying. *Democracy* is a word that has the status of concept. Democracy is defined in our usage as a form of government in which the sovereign power resides in the people and is delegated to freely elected representatives according to particular political rules. (The etymology of the word is insufficient by itself.) Anyone who desires a form of government in which power does not reside in the people and is not delegated to freely elected representatives according to particular political rules, and who nevertheless uses the word *democracy* for this form of government, is a liar. Anyone who tries to enhance his credibility by calling it *people's democracy* lies even more. But he also betrays himself even more. Liars have always betrayed themselves by protesting too much.

THINKING

In Bertolt Brecht's *Caucasian Chalk Circle*, the governor's wife (the bad mother) says at one point, "I *love* the people with their simple, straightforward minds!" That is a lie. We draw our conclusion from the contradiction in the broader context. The governor's wife is led into the courtroom and recoils from the smell of poverty. After the statement above, she continues, "It's only that their smell brings on the migraine." Then she notices Grusche, who is later shown in the chalk circle to be the good mother. "Is that the creature?" she asks (part 2, scene 2).[40] This is not how someone asks who loves the people and their simple, straightforward attitude.

Let's test the lie by Augustine's definition. It is evidently a matter of a false statement ("enuntiatio falsa"). What about the intention to deceive ("voluntas fallendi")? Couldn't the governor's wife be deceiving herself and really believe she loves the people? How is it ever possible to know anything about an intention to deceive? How can we see into the heart of this woman?

Indeed, we are not able to see into her heart, and the possibility of self-deception can never be excluded with full certainty except if the liar confesses under pressure of evidence: "I lied." The governor's wife makes no such confession, and it remains to the judge and to us as spectators to conclude from the indications and evidence: "She lied." This judgment does not, however, simply erase the words of the governor's wife as if she had never said them. It is not the case that it is now completely undecided whether she loves the people or not. Rather, we know definitively: she does *not*. If she had told the truth and not lied, she would have had to say the words "I do *not* love the people (with their simple, straightforward minds)." This sentence remains unsaid. But our judgment that the spoken sentence is a lie and to be condemned as such depends on the assumption that this unspoken sentence— exactly this one and no other—existed in the heart of the governor's wife. Without this assumption, there is no question of lying at all, and no court in the world can distinguish truth from lying.

It is worth pausing at this point to savor our surprise to the full. Haven't I just averred that this lie involves two sentences, not just one? We hear one, and this sentence as such is of no further note. But it is untrue. We don't hear the second sentence, since it remains locked in the speaker's breast. This sentence is true. It states not simply something other than the lying sentence but its exact opposite. This means, linguistically, that the true sentence is identical to the lying one—except for the small particle *not*.

It now appears that lying is a linguistic issue in a much more basic fashion than we had originally assumed. Not only do we lie with the aid of language, we also think the truth with the aid of language. Both lying and truth-telling take place in sentences. And sentences consist of words, whose lexical meanings mutually determine one another into textual meanings and in this way construct sense. Sentences obey the laws of semantics and syntax. Sentences are part of linguistics.

The Augustinian definition of *lie* can now be rectified. Augustine considered it a lie if an intention to deceive stood behind the sentence containing it. Linguistics, however, considers it a lie if behind the (spoken) lying sentence there stands an (unspoken) true sentence, which differs by contradiction, that is, by virtue of the assertion morpheme *yes/no*. Not "double . . . thought," as Augustine calls it,[41] but double speech is the signature of the lie.

The results of this observation concern first what we call thinking, for the unspoken sentence that carries the truth can just as well be called a thought. Now, I have nothing against continuing to call unspoken sentences thoughts, as we have always done. But I do place great weight on the observation that these thoughts or unspoken sentences are made of the same thing as our languages. As natural languages, obviously, not artificial ones. Or in any case as natural languages no less than artificial ones. Thinking, then, obeys linguistic laws before any logical laws that may exist. In particular, it obeys the semantic laws governing the play of determination between the poles of lexical meaning and textual meaning.

Of course, there is no way to prove that thinking is not a completely different process from speaking. But that is unprovable and "unthinkable." The point here is this: we can only talk about lying, and account it a moral flaw in the liar, if we treat thoughts as statements that consist of words and sentences. Only then can thoughts and statements be compared for possible contradictions. One might call this position a hypothesis. But this hypothesis is the basis of our moral order and a good part of our legal order. It is a hypothesis that is verified hundreds of times a day. Its validity is a moral certainty. Its consequences, however, extend far beyond the realm of lying and lay bare the entire problem of speech and thought.

AGAINST ICONOCLASTS

"A deplorable consequence!" Augustine said when he considered that imagistic language in all its forms might perhaps be assigned to the sphere of lying.[42] We had agreed with him, although he had not given any basis for the decision. Now we must return to the topic, and can do so after the semantic presuppositions have been clarified.

To be sure, few people have expressly blamed metaphor—the term we will use here for all linguistic images—for lying. But the reproach is often made implicitly. Deep mistrust of metaphor seems endemic especially to the sciences, and from time to time iconoclasts turn up who promise to purify scientific language of all metaphors, and then everything will be fine and truth will finally come to light. *Comparaison n'est pas raison*: comparisons must give way to reason, they say, and science must express the real in real language. The ideas of the sciences can only be obscured or even distorted by metaphors. A serious scientist writes without metaphors. The further his language is from that beloved of the muses, the more "scientific" is his contribution to knowledge.

We all know them, these iconoclasts and inartistic grumps. If they were at least good scientists! But banishing metaphors does not just mean tearing out the flowers alongside the path to truth; it means, rather, denying oneself the vehicles that speed the journey. Not only can you not write without metaphors, you can't think without them, either. Altogether, the idea that metaphors are less precise than other words is a rumor utterly without basis. Semantics has something to say about this.

Return for a moment to the distinction between lexical meaning and textual meaning. The lexical meaning of the isolated word is determined, by the context, to the speaker's textual meaning and becomes part of the overall sense. This is every bit as true for metaphor, and thus for every form of verbal image. Metaphors are made of words. They obey, therefore, the principles of semantics. Metaphors show more clearly than other words do that a simple semantics of words, without the supplement of text semantics, results in, at best, half the truth of this discipline. After all, a word by itself can never be a metaphor. *Fire*, taken entirely without context or situation, is always the standard word with the known lexical meaning. Only context can turn this word into a metaphor. (Naturally, the context can, as always, be replaced by a situation.) *Fire of passion* would be a metaphor, to remain with this example. Clearly, it is no longer fire in the physical sense of the word, but some manifestation of passion. What has actually changed here? Has the word *fire*, as a metaphor, taken on a new lexical meaning?

No, we wouldn't want to say that. The lexical meaning of a word is always the same, whether or not the word is used as a metaphor. But if metaphor requires context as the condition of its genesis, then it is subject not to the semantics of the isolated word but to that of text, with its play of determination between the poles of lexical meaning and textual meaning. Determination doesn't eliminate meaning; it only restricts it. Exactly the same thing happens in the kind of context that turns a word into a metaphor. It too determines the word, as every context does. But it determines it in a special fashion. Whereas an ordinary context determines a word within its lexical meaning, in a metaphorical context the determination takes place outside the lexical meaning. As a result, a tension develops between the lexical meaning and the textual meaning, which now is located not within but outside the lexical meaning. This tension constitutes the charm of metaphor.

What has been said can be clarified with reference to the principles of information theory. Information is the reduction of possibilities. Every lexical meaning is information to the extent that it excludes some of the previously available possibilities. Determination through context is also information, since it excludes some of the possibilities inherent in the lexical meaning. But for individual words the concept "information" has two dimensions. On the one hand it refers to the world—that is, the totality of possibilities—that seeks to become language. The verbal sign, when it is heard, tells us what is now excluded from possibility. A second dimension applies, meanwhile, to the verbal signs to be expected in the course of communication. The totality of word sequences theoretically possible is in fact already restricted once the first word is spoken. Many words are now more or less unlikely for the communicative sequence. They are no longer expected. That is a reduction in possibilities—not certain, of course, but probable. In language, this preliminary information about the determination to be expected is also a reality. The word *fire* brings with it an expected determination that can be—roughly—characterized with further talk of fireplaces, flame, light, ruins, ashes, or the like. We expect the determination to lead in a particular direction that can be evoked by a bundle of associations. (If we had to decipher an illegible text in which only the word *fire* could be made out, then we would let our decoding intuitions play first in the direction just indicated.)

Most of the time, our expectations about the determination are not disappointed. Thus, for example, when we hear Erichtho in the Classical Walpurgis Night in act 2 of Goethe's *Faust, Part II*—"Watch fires are glowing, as they scatter red flames"[43]—the context does correspond to the word *fire*, as was to be expected. But if the language jumps to an entirely different sphere instead of staying close to the word *fire*, that can't be foreseen from the word, and our expected determination is disappointed. "In meinen Adern welches Feuer! / In meinem Herzen welche Glut!" (In my veins what fire! / In my heart what heat!): in these lines from Goethe's poem "Willkommen und Abschied" we anticipate a different, admittedly imprecise, textual meaning from the one actually created by the context. We have to revise our expectation and are thereby slightly shaken in our calculations of the truth. That is precisely the metaphorical tension; and, furthermore, the more narrowly the real determination misses the expected one, the greater it is. A strong tradition of metaphorical usage, however, such as exists with the image *fire of love*, reduces the metaphor's tension.[44]

So there is necessarily a deception attached to metaphor. But is this deception in the nature of lying? Surely not. For it is only a deception of expectation, actually a disappointment—it does not create an illusion but undoes one. We had taken the probability for certainty and are now startled out of our serene expectation. But once the metaphorical determination has taken place outside our original horizon of expectation, everything is all right again, and the textual meaning of the metaphor is just as narrow, precise, individual, and concrete as any other textual meaning. In this respect, metaphors are no different from other words in texts.

There is, therefore, no reason to mistrust metaphor. It diverges in only one small peculiarity from other words in texts, and this peculiarity does not place it beyond the bounds of the general dialectic of lexical and textual meaning. Hence it makes no sense to say that the meanings of words are proper but that those of metaphors are not. As long as words are without context, they are neither proper nor improper but are primarily instructions about what to expect. Robert Musil writes, "Even 'dog' is something no one can imagine; it is only a token of particular dogs and doggy attributes."[45] Only after the textual meaning has been determined by a word's context can its propriety or lack thereof be questioned. And by then it is almost superfluous. Of course, you can say that a particular word "properly" leads you to expect a particular direction of determination, and this expectation is then either fulfilled or not fulfilled. But the condition of unambiguous communication is always fulfilled; otherwise language couldn't afford metaphors at all. One can express oneself just as clearly and exactly with metaphors as with other words. It simply is not the case that language with imagery lies over a stratum of proper meaning like a pretty but completely dispensable carpet of flowers. Metaphors are as proper as anyone could want. They cannot be replaced by direct expressions; and even if it is occasionally possible, it shouldn't be done, because then something proper would be being replaced by something improper. Periphrases are always weaker than what they replace. All words should be equally acceptable when they are used in texts—those in expected contexts and those in the unexpected contexts that constitute metaphors.

There is no lying attached to metaphors. Language doesn't lie, and we don't lie when we speak in images. Our thoughts come pure and undistorted to others, whether we construct them from regular words or from metaphors, because we are always constructing them as texts, and the same context that creates the metaphors also guarantees that the metaphors correspond to the textual meaning of the speaker. As long as the pole of textual meaning is reached, the speech is as unambiguous as the speaker pleases.

YES AND NO

Isolated words are fictitious words. Only words in texts are real words. The play of determination in sentence and text belongs to semantics. Thus have we understood semantics. Does that leave any space at all for syntax? The traditional definition of syntax says it takes as its object the linkage of words in the sentence. That is a bad definition, like all definitions based only on etymology (*syn-taxis*). The linkage of word meanings, such that they mutually limit one another and jointly construct the sense of the sentence, cannot be the object of any branch of the discipline but semantics.

It is best to begin with the question of what a sentence is. Utterances, entirely without regard to their semantic information, have the status of sentences. Words can be piled upon words, even in meaningful configurations, without necessarily forming a sentence. The opening line of Weber's *Der Freischütz*, "Schöner, grüner Jungfernkranz" (Lovely, green bridal wreath), for example: this utterance offers us lexical meanings, and these meanings determine one another by their simple juxtaposition into textual meanings and result in sense. But the utterance is not a sentence. "We weave your bridal wreath" is, on the contrary, a sentence. The difference is evident. The (finite) verb makes the sentence. Yet the verb does not derive this power from its semantic information. The noun *weaving* would preserve the semantic information of the verb, but with it the utterance would no longer be a sentence.

In this situation, syntax can help. Syntax can be understood as the theory of sentences insofar as it takes for its object everything that makes an utterance a sentence. At its deepest level, this is the same as what makes a verb finite. For verbs are different from all other word classes in that their core of meaning is surrounded by a whole troop of morphemes that determine them in a particular manner, namely, toward the speech situation. First in our example comes the personal morpheme *we*. The personal morpheme relates the lexical meaning of the verb, and thereby the sense of the whole sentence, to the basic situation of all speaking, the communication triangle I: you: he/she. The plural form *we* also establishes the site of the information in this model of communication. In addition, the verb has a tense morpheme (in our example, the present). It too determines the meaning of the verb in a special fashion. It specifies whether the speech is to be related directly to the situation in which it is spoken or only indirectly, as perhaps narrative about an occurrence at a distance. (Tense has nothing to do with time.)[46] That is also a determination of the speech situation and includes simultaneously what grammars call *mode*. And then there is another morpheme that is often overlooked because it is so obvious. In our example, it is the zero morpheme, and it indicates *yes*. The morpheme *not* could be there instead, and then the sense of the entire sentence would be turned into its opposite. As I said, this is so obvious that it is almost banal to mention it. But it seems to me worth considering that our languages are constructed such that there is no sentence that cannot be determined by a morpheme, audible or not, into *yes* or *no*. Let's call this morpheme the *assertion morpheme*.

It might in fact be correct to overlook or ignore the assertion morpheme if it weren't for its odd parallelism with the determination of verbs. The assertion morpheme is as tightly bound to the verb as are the personal morpheme and the tense morpheme. All three types of determination must be present if the utterance is to be a sentence, regardless of the semantic information it might contain. These three types of determination must have some special weight, since they alone determine whether an expression is a sentence. For personal morphemes and tense morphemes, the special weight derives from the fact that they connect the verb to its speech situation—indeed, to that situation in its fundamental form, as a model of communication. It is hard to avoid the surmise that perhaps the assertion morpheme also links the meaning of the verb, and, with it, the sense of the sentence, to the speech situation.

At this point, we can expect logic to object strongly. After all, logic has created its truth tables for *yes* and *no*, and it doesn't give the least hint that anything like the speech situation needs to be taken into account. But then there are other linguistic aspects that logic does not take into account. Among the three types of determination constitutive of sentences in natural languages, logic makes a choice that seems arbitrary and unmotivated from the point of view of language. Logic pays the personal determinant extraordinarily careful attention, which cannot but strike the linguist as rank favoritism. As "subject" (after a neutralizing normalization to the third person), it is elevated even above the "predicate" and made the pillar, or at least one of the two pillars, of utterances. Isn't that too much honor for a determining morpheme? A linguist might expect the tense morpheme to receive equivalent attention, since it is so clearly parallel to the personal morpheme in actual languages. Far from it. The tense determinant is all but completely eliminated, on the grounds that logic deals only with timeless statements. But, in truth, the tense determinant cannot be suppressed. Without it, there can be no sentences, even in the artificial language of logic. But it too can be normalized and thereby neutralized. Logicians do that with the (unreflected) convention of always using the present and not thinking any more about it. The assertion determinant, finally, is treated extensively, as is well known.

Linguists may well wonder about logicians' principles of selection and emphasis with regard to the determinants of the verb. But of course logic is free to make its own rules. We mustn't be surprised, then, that its results are only rarely relevant to linguistics.

How are we to understand the fact that the assertion determinant of verbs refers to the speech situation in a way that is analogous to the way the person and tense determinants do? In this context, it is helpful to remember the two thought experiments that—independently of one another—led to the discovery of the speech situation. The first is linked to the often misunderstood concept of behavior. I describe it here, following Leonard Bloomfield's book *Language* (1933). A speech act, Bloomfield argues, does not take place in a no-man's-land but in a real-life situation where before, during, and after speaking there is also action. Speech acts and action acts are entirely interchangeable. If we operate with the—rather limited, to be sure—schema of a game of stimulus and response, where each response functions as a new stimulus, then we get long stimulus-response chains in which linguistic and nonlinguistic acts are mixed. Bloomfield, if he applied this schema to our example sentence, would refuse to interpret the sentence, "We weave you a bridal wreath," in isolation. He would ask: What actually evoked this sentence? What is the linguistic or nonlinguistic stimulus? And how does the chain proceed?

The second thought experiment comes from recent philosophy. It is linked to the concepts of dialectics. I shall describe it by using an essay of Hans-Georg Gadamer.[47] Gadamer emphasizes first in this essay the special status of the propositional statement or judgment as an utterance that makes "the reason of things themselves" communicable.[48] That is traditional philosophizing. But then Gadamer turns to dialectics. We miss the truth of the statement, Gadamer argues, if we consider only its content. A statement has presuppositions that it does not articulate. It is motivated (this is the *stimulus* of the behaviorists), and by a question. The question takes priority over the statement. Elicited by a question, the statement itself is another question and elicits another statement. And so there develops a long chain of questions, and of answers that are themselves questions, and questions that are again answers. Dialectics inserts itself ahead of logic.

The correspondences between the "behaviorist" thought model of the American linguist and the dialectical one of the German philosopher are striking. They hardly need to be harmonized. We might add that Gadamer took the next step from this dialectical foundation to hermeneutics. He writes: "The question as answer has itself in its general propositional character a hermeneutical function. They are both an address."[49] In this context, the personal determinant of the speech situation is restored to its rightful place. Philosophy seems to (re-)discover language.

These reflections may also cast light on the assertion determinant. On the one hand, the assertion determinant must be very important, just like the person and tense determinants, since it must be present for every verb. Not only can it not be left out, it can't even be thought away. On the other hand, it was difficult to establish a necessary connection between *yes* and *no* as verb determinants and the speech situation. This difficulty evaporates, however, if the speech situation is not viewed as a static constellation. As both the behaviorist and the dialectical-hermeneutic models show, it is instead a dynamic constellation in which we proceed from question to answer, answer to question, or— if one prefers the other terminology—from stimulus to response, response to stimulus.

Surely, though, the choice between stimulus and question, response and answer, is more than a difference in terminology. It seems to me that the philosopher Gadamer has a better—which means, in this context, a more linguistic— terminology than the linguist Bloomfield. So we will follow him. But it remains to say what a question is. That is relatively easy, in grammatical terms. Grammar distinguishes, as we all know, between total questions ("Do you remember?") and partial questions ("What do you remember?"). It is obvious that total questions refer to the *yes/no* of the assertion morpheme. Partial questions do not, or at least not directly. But I would like to take the concept question in the broad sense Gadamer uses when he says that every answer is simultaneously another question for a new answer. Taking all the grammatical kinds of questions together with this kind, we can say: a question, with respect to the answer that follows it, offers less information about its situation, but not none at all. The statement can also be made positively. A question expresses preliminary knowledge. Only someone who already knows something can ask a question. Naturally, something is missing in the information (rising intonation is often the prosodic equivalent of this lack), but what's missing is only a supplement. This missing supplement can be large or small; that distinguishes questions from one another. But it can never be so large that the answer cannot assume some knowledge in the questioner. It also cannot be so small that the answer cannot add new information to it. The minimum of supplementary information comes with a total question. Nothing is missing here except agreement (*yes*) or denial (*no*). It is a *yes* or a *no* to the preliminary information. This also applies to situations in which the preliminary information doesn't even have the character of a question in the grammatical sense. Gadamer is correct to include such situations. In a speech situation, it matters little for the dialectical value of preliminary information whether or not there is a rise in intonation or a recognized question pronoun. What matters is that a sentence does not normally send information into an informational vacuum but instead supplements given preliminary information. That is a basic fact of linguistics, more precisely, of syntax. Its expression in language is the assertion morpheme *yes/no*. It is a morpheme that language has created in order to set the new information provided by a speaker into relationship with the interlocutor's preliminary information. Its function, prior to any logical one, is dialectical, and that means syntactic.

All three necessary determinants of the verb go to the

heart of the speech situation. At the same time, they reveal the three crucial aspects of the speech situation. We can identify them with linguistic concepts: *person, tense, assertion*. Before all the other, secondary tasks that develop from it, syntax is the investigation of person, tense, and assertion as the manner in which lexical meanings are connected to the speech situation. And *sentence* refers to all utterances in which this connection is fully established.

With these reflections, we are now in a position to add a syntax of lying to our previously sketched semantics of lying. "There are many kinds of lies," says Augustine, "all of which, indeed, we should detest uniformly. There is no lie which is not contrary to truth. For, just as light and darkness, piety and impiety, justice and inequity, sin and integrity, sanity and imbecility, life and death—even so are truth and falsehood contrary to one another."[50] Like *yes* and *no*, we might add. Because lying is, finally, always related to *yes* or *no*. At least, that is true for lying in its evil essence. This is the lie that answers the total question. Hence we could call it the total lie. It assumes the interlocutor has a maximum of preliminary information, for which only the decision of whether it should be confirmed or rejected is still missing. Confirmation or rejection are given with *yes* or *no*. Consequently, the assertion morpheme is used to lie. This is typical of the great lies that have turned the course of the world to evil.

Hitler lied in this manner. During the Sudeten crisis of 1938, Hitler insisted in a public speech on September 26, 1938, regarding his negotiations with British Prime Minister Chamberlain, "I assured him that the German people only want peace. . . . I further assured him, and repeat it here, that Germany—once this problem is solved—has no further territorial problem."[51] We know today from the documents, and could have known it from thousands of clues then, that Hitler's Germany had no desire for peace. The secret order to the generals of May 30, 1938, was in force: "It is my inalterable decision to wipe out Czechoslovakia in the foreseeable future. . . . Appropriate preparations are to be made immediately."[52] The course of history has shown that this decision was in fact not changed. Czechoslovakia was wiped out, and then there were further "territorial problems," until the whole territory came under German occupation.

History knows no worse lies than those of Hitler. For that reason, it is important to study them, and also with the tools of linguistics. It does not suffice to establish that the statements of the public speech and those of the secret commando affair cannot be reconciled, and that the public statements are lies, since the secret ones have been shown to be true. It is more important to see that Hitler's speech was not spoken into thin air. It was a speech for people inside and outside Germany who were listening with intense expectations and fears. The listeners were already informed, rightly or wrongly, about the man and his country. There had been references to "territorial problems" for a long time, and for a long time the anxious question had already been, War or peace? Hitler was not simply creating a self-contained communication about peace and borders in Europe but was answering in these sentences, in semantically veiled fashion, the terrible question "War—yes or no? Aggression—yes or no?" Everyone listening to Hitler already had the preliminary information to know that war and aggression were the real issues. His statements answered these questions. They denied the preliminary information with a clear *no*: "War?—No. Aggression?—No." In this speech situation, that is the true site of the lie anxiously heard over the radio and still clearly present to many of us. Which words enter into the service of the lie, whether "territorial problems" replaces "aggression," is of secondary significance here. It was not a matter of new information, in contrast to a previously existing absence of information, but for all participants it was a matter of the decisive supplement to what they already knew—whether there would be peace or not. Every word was doubtless heard, but only the *yes* or *no* was listened for. Only one morpheme was listened for. In this morpheme, truth was made false. The terrible, evil, total lie is syntactic in nature; it falsifies the sense at the decisive point where speech and world come together, in the speech situation.

Not every lie is a total lie, of course, and not every lie is as radically evil as this one. The problem of lying would not be a *magna quaestio* if black and white were always so clearly distributed. There are half-lies, and there are those minor deviations from the truth that are perhaps so dangerous because they are so hard to recognize. Finally, there are the thousand kinds of diplomatic lies, and not only among diplomats. But there is no point in attempting a casuistics of lying. The morality of other centuries has already embarrassed itself with that. Linguistics doesn't need to repeat such errors.

IRONY

"Socrates was the first to introduce irony." Thus reads one of the theses that Kierkegaard defends in his dissertation.[53] Socrates the teacher of truth: did he teach us to lie? After all, in Wolfgang Kayser we can find the sentence, "With irony the opposite is meant from what is said in words."[54] This agrees fairly well with the linguistic definition of lying developed above: a spoken sentence hides an unspoken sentence that differs from the first by the assertion morpheme. So it is not surprising when Frédéric Paulhan begins his definition of irony thus: "Irony is a form of lying."[55] Yet Proudhon is really more correct when he calls the "goddess" Irony, in a hymnic invocation, the "mistress of truth."[56] Truth and lie are not opposed in irony.

Irony (*eironeia*) was known to the Greeks who came before Socrates. But it was considered a more or less disgraceful dissimulation, indeed a reductive one. Goethe's term *Kleintun* [playing small] might be used to translate the Greek concept of irony.[57] Even someone who understated the value of his property to the tax authority counted as an ironist. That was, at bottom, just as much lie and deception as was dissimulation upward, or exaggerating. Aristotle has to admit, in the *Ethics*, that exaggerating and understating are actually equally distanced from the golden mean of truthfulness. They are vices. But then, in a gesture that basically cannot be reconciled with his ethical system, he adds the reservation, "Mock-modest people, who understate things, seem more attractive in character than boasters." We learn immediately why Aristotle is so inconsistently sympathetic—namely, Socrates' name drops. For the sake of the ironic philosopher who pretends to know nothing, Aristotle ups the value of irony.[58]

The revalorization of irony continued through the ages. Preserved by rhetoric in Latin antiquity and the Latin Middle Ages, discovered as a narrative stance by the epic in the Renaissance and the eighteenth century, irony was canonized by the Romantics as a metaphysical habitus and survived in modern literature even after Romanticism was deromanticized. Poets love it more than ever as the unequal sister of imagination.

Irony covers a broad range, from the everyday irony in conversation on the street to Friedrich Schlegel's "transcendental buffoonery."[59] In all its forms, however, irony is fundamentally different from Greek irony before Socrates. That was understatement, nothing more. Since Socrates, and in our entire literary tradition, irony has been something more. Part of irony is the irony signal: one understates and simultaneously lets on that one is understating. Of course, it is deception, but the deception is identified as such. The irony signal is just as necessary for irony as understatement is. Only together do they turn the *dissimulatio*, to use Cicero's terms, into a *dissimulatio urbana*, which is free of any moral flaw.[60] Ever since irony separated from *eironeia*, plain understatement unmarked as irony has been ethically even more disgraceful than it was in Greek times, when the understater had the benefit of the Greek respect for cunning. A modern understater is Molière's Tartuffe, and no one any longer respects his deceitfulness as cunning.

If it is permissible for linguistics to take an interest in lying, then surely it must be permissible for it to reflect on irony. For if, indeed, irony absolutely requires the addition of an irony signal in order to be considered irony at all, the term *signal* immediately brings to mind the semiotic function of language. There are all sorts of irony signals. It might be the wink of an eye, a cough, vocal emphasis, a special intonation, an accumulation of bombastic expressions, extreme metaphors, overlong sentences, verbal repetitions, or—in printed texts—italics and quotation marks. They are all signals, that is to say, signs. Most of the time, and this is of course of special interest to linguists, they are verbal signs: words, sounds, or prosodic oddities. In written texts, the various kinds of irony signals constitute an important chapter in the stylistics of irony.

Let's return for a moment to our communication model. Language is communication and a code shared by a speaker and a hearer. Whatever particular language is being spoken (German, French, Russian) is the code, which is actualized by separate speech acts, that is, spoken or written texts. Ironic language is also such a speech act between a speaker and a hearer. But when the speaker is the ignorant Socrates and the hearer the know-it-all priest Euthyphro, as in Plato's famous dialogue, there is a gradient of irony between the overstating Euthyphro and the understating Socrates, who says to the priest: "Well then, admirable Euthyphro, the best thing I can do is to become your pupil."[61] This irony gradient is expressed in words. Does it also correspond to thoughts? The first question is, whose thoughts? Clearly, it corresponds to what Euthyphro thinks; a little later, when Socrates ironically reminds Euthyphro again that he is accustomed to characterize himself as the expert in divine affairs, Euthyphro interrupts him and affirms: "Yes, Socrates, I say so, and I tell the truth."[62] But it evidently does not correspond to Socrates' thoughts (nor to ours). For the understatement of the philosopher is only an aspect of that philosophical midwifery that does not distribute truth but wants it to be discovered. Hence Socrates seems to allow himself to be taught so that the teacher can notice from his pupil's penetrating questions how poor his teaching is and how much he himself needs instruction. After the ironic destruction of his false and conceited opinion comes the shared construction of clear concepts and true knowledge. It turns out that the philosopher's ignorance is in fact a deception, an understatement. Socrates is not only, in truth, superior to the Sophists and other braggarts but also aware of his superiority, at least on the basis of his oracle and his daimon. But he hides his mental superiority behind his understated words. Musil on the topic: "Socratic is: to pretend ignorance. Modern: to be ignorant."[63]

If there were no more to say, we would have to sum up here and say, yes, Socrates' irony is a lie. At best, one might add that Socratic irony, as a pedagogical tool, serves a wholesome end and is justified by its noble purpose. In Augustinian terms, the intention to deceive is balanced and neutralized by the intention to heal.

But the linguistic analysis of irony is only half complete. We have not yet taken account of the irony signal, which belongs to irony just as much as understatement does. If we imagine it for a moment as emphatic intonation, the irony signal is a linguistic sign that accompanies spoken language. It is so constituted that it can be both heard and overheard. It involves a code that is not identical to the general grammatical code and that is shared only by those with wit. Those who are semicultured or conceited overhear it, and the irony signal misses its mark. That, however, is the fault not of the speaker but of the listener.

The linguistic analysis of irony is simplified if we imagine the elementary model of communication from which we began broadened to an elementary model of irony by the addition of a third person to the speaker and the listener. In the ironic dialogue between Socrates and Euthyphro, we might think of Plato as the third. We are confident that Plato, as witness to the dialogue, understood the irony signal. As author of the Socratic dialogues—perhaps even as inventor of an irony only ascribed to Socrates, a contested point[64]—he has been careful to transmit the irony signals. That isn't so simple; we know from our own experience with ironic language how many irony signals are carried in nuances and are not accessible to being recorded with letters of the alphabet. Irony signals that are to work in written and printed texts have to be translated in various ways from a spoken language, rich in nuances, into a different medium of expression. The words must be chosen so that they cannot be read in anything but an ironic tone. That is an encoding and a renewed decoding of the irony signal. Here is a sentence from the *Euthyphro* as an example. The speaker is Socrates, who has just had to accept Euthyphro's praise for following him so well. Now Socrates says, "My friend, . . . I have my heart set on your wisdom, and give my mind to it, so that nothing you say shall be lost."[65] One must imagine Socrates making his answer in an unctuously pompous tone of voice. Yet unless the author of the dialogue wants to include stage directions, this tone cannot be reproduced in written signs. But it is preserved in the arrangement of the text itself and translated into adjectives ("great desire," "all my thoughts"), in a metaphor ("the crumbs of wisdom"), and in a saccharine address ("my friend"). As a result, the reader cannot help retranslating these stylistic irony signals back into precisely the intonation of voice that Socrates must originally have used to signal his irony.

Plato's text suggests that the irony signal has not penetrated to the smug priest. To be sure, he notices how Socrates runs him around in circles with his questions, but he does not notice that the ignorance of his interlocutor is an act. The code of the irony signals is closed to him. But Plato, the third person in the speech situation, has understood them. And he has transmitted them to us, the readers of his dialogues. If we understand them as he has entrusted them to the written dialogue, then we too become witnesses to the conversation and are present as a third person. The linguistic communications emanating from Socrates travel, therefore, in two different directions.

It is as if they split; one chain of information goes to the listener being addressed and says *yes* while a second, simultaneous chain goes to a third person also being addressed and says *no*. This chain of information is formed from the irony signals. Its code is a secret code of those who are clever and well-meaning. "Who hath ears to hear, let him hear" (Matthew 13:9).

The situation we have been discussing, with speaker, listener, and third person, is a model. It does not mean that irony is possible only when a third person is literally present. It may well be that no third person is there. That does not exclude the possibility of irony where it is necessary. The speaker cannot omit the irony signals or else he will degrade himself into a hypocrite. It's a shame that no one is there to pick up the lost signals. A shame, but not hopeless. It is possible, for example, to return to the situation in narrative and now, in the presence of a different third person, have the delayed irony signals find a listener. That is generally not very satisfying, because the irony no longer carries any risk, but sometimes, when ears are all too deaf, there's no choice.

In the last analysis, even a listener is not indispensable for realizing the model. There is self-irony, where the ironic speaker is his own listener and object. Self-irony is a marginal case, but perhaps also at the same time irony's purest realization. It is necessary, naturally, to keep in mind that the third person is also always present in self-irony. Again, it is we ourselves. Anyone who ironizes himself becomes a spectacle to himself.

Occasionally, at its highest moments, all the models of irony collapse into one, as Robert Musil describes it: "Irony is representing a cleric in such a fashion that you have also caught a Bolshevik. Representing an idiot so that the author suddenly feels: that's me as well."[66]

"POETS ARE LIARS"

In Homer, lying is still unproblematic. Odysseus, the hero of many wiles, is praised by gods and men whenever he pulls off a whopper. It is a measure of wit or *ingenium* to master the art of lying. Not even the gods shun lying and deception, and they model this art for humans. Homer's epics, which preserve all these lies, are a school for liars.

The philosophers quickly took offense. Especially Plato, who charged poets with lying when they alleged that the gods lie. The ideal state had no place for such lies, and poets would not be permitted to lead the young astray with them. With Plato's expulsion of lying, the lie became a literary problem and took on a significance extending far beyond popular fairy tales about lying. That is already clear in Lucian of Samosata. In his dialogue "The Liar" we have a liar and a skeptic, and the skeptic has been put on his guard by the lies of a Herodotus and a Homer. Fortunately, poets have not given up lying, and our states are not so ideal that poets are forbidden to lie. Indeed, poets have discovered lying as a literary theme and developed it into its own very consistent province of literature. To measure its full extent would take us too far afield. For a linguistics of lying, it is nevertheless essential to describe a few of the basic structures of the European literature of lying. They are linguistic as well as literary.

Let's imagine we are watching Goldoni's comedy *The Liar* (1750) on stage. We have entered the theater with the expectation, aroused by the title, that we will encounter a liar. All kinds of characters come on: Doctor Balanzoni and his daughter, Ottavio, Florindo, Brighella, Pantalone, Lelio, Arlecchino, and many others, all the way down to the gondoliers. The connoisseur will recognize many of these figures as types from commedia dell'arte, but that is not the issue. With or without this knowledge, the spectator still has to figure out which of these characters is the liar. In fact, comic technique demands—and the author of comedies must observe this—that the spectator recognize the liar as such long before the entire house of lies collapses at the end. His laughter, after all, depends on a certain information gradient in his favor. So how does he learn that Lelio is the liar?

It comes out right at the beginning—Goldoni is careful to secure his effects—from the mouth of the servant Arlecchino, with whom Lelio appears in the second scene. In asides or in dialogue with his master, Arlecchino makes clear to the audience that it should expect bald-faced lies. All Lelio does is downplay a little: "These are not lies, but witty inventions" (act 1, scene 4).[67] This relatively crude

65

effect runs through the whole play, and the spectator thus constantly receives very clear *lying signals*.

This is the essential key for all the literature of lying. The literature of lying, including literature about the figure of the liar, is shot through with a profusion of lying signals that, moreover, have been inherited through the ages with remarkable consistency. They are topoi of form and content that don't even need to be transmitted through conscious learning; instead, they turn up as if on their own whenever someone tries to write a story about lying. Lying signals are every bit as necessary for literary lying as irony signals are for irony. They are a part of the information, and for everyone with the ears to hear, they turn the information into its opposite. Lying speech, to be sure, asserts the opposite of secret thoughts, but the complete information, lying speech plus lying signal, is the equivalent of secret thoughts. Lying speech and lying signal cancel one another out. A literary lie accompanied by a lying signal no longer amounts to a nonliterary lie.

In the Goldoni scene just referred to, lying speech and lying signals separate into the responses of liar and servant. It is a literary convention of confidant scenes that this is possible. The confidants function as pieces of the protagonist's self. But in Goldoni there is in addition a rich inventory of other and more subtle lying signals. Above all there is the lying signal par excellence: the protestation of truthfulness. Lucian had already titled a tale of lying *True History*, and in modern times Cocteau still has his liar in the monologue "The Liar" begin: "I want to tell the truth.

I like the truth."[68] That is also how to understand Lelio when he insists: "Heaven forbid that I should speak falsely. I am incapable of altering the truth in the slightest degree. From my youth upwards there is not a person who can reproach me with even the most trivial taradiddle. Ask my servant" (act 1, scene 11).[69] Here we see a whole bundle of secondary motifs around the classical protestation of truth. The liar swears sacred oaths and is prepared, if necessary, to fall down dead if his word is not true. To protest truthfulness is simultaneously to deny lying or even the capacity to lie. Protesting truthfulness also involves invoking firsthand witnesses or, in the absence of false witnesses, claiming to have seen or heard an event oneself. If none of that works, the liar switches from defense to attack and quickly accuses others of lying. This is what Schiller calls the "brazen confidence of lying," and Goldoni's Lelio has it, too. It expresses itself in a boundless delight in inventing details for one's lies. Goldoni's liar challenges the best journalists of Europe "to invent a fact more circumstantially" (act 2, scene 12).[70] Exact names and numbers are especially crucial for precise detail; the liar spares none. It's bad if he gets them muddled. "Your memory should be good, once you have lied," we hear already in Corneille's *The Liar*.[71] If you come to grief with one lie, then you just lie yourself right out with an even bigger one. The "champion liar" shoves a great mountain of lies ahead of himself, and it keeps growing the longer he keeps at it, and the more he gets caught in a lie. Partial confession of a lie is only a springboard to new inventions and is invoked as the profession of truth for a new and bigger lie.

All these are lying signals, and it hardly requires literary training to recognize them. A little knowledge of human nature will do.[72] Literature builds on elementary human psychology and intensifies its elements to motifs. Anyone utterly lacking in knowledge of human nature will be at sea in the literature of lying because he will miss the lying signals. He will then have the experience of a recent Lucian commentator, who after almost two thousand years still buys into one of the lover of lying's lies. The lover of lying, Eukrates, insists that he doesn't quite know about one point in his tall tales. The learned commentator remarks in a footnote that this is another example proving that Lucian described his Eukrates from real life.[73] No, dear commentator, it only proves that Lucian understood the art of lying signals. If you give a hundred details and then say at the hundred and first that you are no longer certain, you validate the other hundred in a way that can't be topped. Here begins the refinement of lying signals.

In Lucian there are other lying signals not readily available to the theater. In the dialogue "The Liar" the skeptic finds himself in a large company of skilled liars. They tell one another stories bursting with lies. The pleasure of lying shows in their faces. This is a fundamental situation for literary lying. People tell one another tall tales. It is a circle, as in Boccaccio, but the effects are coarser. Everyone in turn has to try to top the lies of the others. The speech situation is that of a contest. Stories are introduced by devaluing the preceding one: "That's nothing—just listen to my story. . . ." The winner is the one who invents the most outrageous lies. He is the champion liar. In fairy tales there is often a variant of this speech situation, when the king of lies promises the hand of his daughter in marriage to the best liar. Thus are formed dynasties and ruling houses in the kingdom of lying.

Lying signals can also be found in the content of lying stories. The literary lie has its preferred hunting grounds. Love, war, sea journeys, and hunting have their special lore—all dangerous activities in which the issue is success. "The telling of amorous adventures lacks flavour without a spice of romance," says Goldoni's Lelio (act 1, scene 15), and he should know.[74] Once some framework has established the expectation of lying, as the title often does in lying literature, simply the choice of one of these themes is a lying signal. With these themes, it is a pleasure to be deceived.

There is yet another land where lies are at home. I don't mean Crete, whose inhabitants, according to a famous sophism, are all liars. (But it is a Cretan who says so, and so it probably isn't true. On the other hand, this Cretan lied, and so the other Cretans could be liars, too.[75]) I mean the land we also call "the world upside down."[76] One of its provinces is called the land of Cockaigne, and there is a story about it that begins: "I want to tell you a story. I saw two roasted pigeons fly. . . ." In ordinary life, roasted pigeons don't usually fly into our mouths; they do in the land of Cockaigne, where everything works differently. It is always like that in the world upside down. Everything has been turned on its head: fish fly, birds creep; sheep are wild, lions tame; youths rest, and old men dance; it snows roses and rains cool wine. We already know: it doesn't really snow roses or rain wine, but we don't let the lying signal of the series of impossibilities scare us off from following the lying narrator into the land of absurdities when he begins: "It was dark, the moon shone bright, / The meadow green lay deep in snow, / When a carriage swift as light / Around the bend did slowly go."[77] We enter this land and greet its inhabitants with a smile related to that of the augurers. It is the smile by which the members of a college of liars recognize one another, a lying signal for initiates, a riddle for dummies and serious folk.

There have always been voices inflicting seriousness on all of literature by declaring it a land of lies. We wouldn't even mention such voices were Plato's not among them. It is the voice of a philosopher, and so the reproach that poetry lies also implies that philosophy speaks the language of reality, poetry that of unreality. Just as, in lying, the spoken sentence covers over a thought sentence, so the words of the poets, it is claimed, clothe the thoughts of the philosophers. In comparison to the truth of philosophy, poetry is lying, or at least tarnished truth, and a laborious philosophical exegesis is necessary to bring the fiction of the poets (with great effort) into harmony with the pure doctrine of the teachers of wisdom.

Blessed he who has this faith! Nothing can be done for him; the muses have denied him a different insight. Herder writes: "Only a fool would confuse poetry and lying."[78] And Nietzsche notes: "Art treats *illusion as illusion*; therefore it does not wish to deceive; it *is true*."[79] Anyone who doesn't believe that will also not be convinced by a linguistics of lying. If, however, he has accepted the preceding reflections, then a linguistics of lying can at least relieve him of some scruples. No one is deceived by literature. Not because there is no intention to deceive; poets do have the intention of making things up. But whenever literature lies, the lying signals are also always there. Literature does present itself as literature. All the traditional markers of genre are also signals that this spoken or printed text is literature, not truth. And the genre that must come most often under suspicion of lying, the fairy tale, also has the clearest generic markers. Even a child can understand them.

But one point must be ceded to those hostile to literature. There did come a time in the history of literature when literature seemed to lose its way. Literature insisted that it wanted to deliver truth. Fine, nothing new in that. The signal was well known from the long tradition of lying literature. It could be interpreted to mean that literature would now invent especially outrageous lies. But, lo and behold, that was not what was meant. Literature did not want to invent bigger lies; it wanted to articulate deeper truths. It wanted to be "realistic." That was irritating; suddenly the signals no longer worked properly. Since that time, everything has become much more complicated in literature, and since then the liars—I mean the real liars—have realized that they can press literature into the service of their dishonest purposes. Literature in the service of lying is lying. But, also since that time, every work of literature that rejects the service of lying is truth, and—in Brecht's words—truth that "is worth the telling."[80]

NOTES

1. My positions on linguistics are to be found primarily in my book *Sprache in Texten* (Stuttgart: Klett, 1976) and in my grammars, *Textgrammatik der französischen Sprache* (Stuttgart: Klett, 1982)—in French, *Grammaire textuelle du français* (Paris: Didier, 1989)—and *Textgrammatik der deutschen Sprache* (Mannheim: Duden, 1993).

2. Friedrich Nietzsche, *Beyond Good and Evil*, trans. Marianne Cowan (Chicago: Regnery, 1955), 73–74.

3. For more on Freud in this respect, see my book *Lethe: The Art and Critique of Forgetting*, trans. Steven Rendall (Ithaca: Cornell University Press, 2004), 132–36.

4. Peter Weiss, *The Investigation*, trans. Jon Swan and Ulu Grosbard, rev. Robert Cohen, in *Marat/Sade, The Investigation, and the Shadow of the Body of the Coachman*, ed. Robert Cohen (New York: Continuum, 1998).

5. Molière, *Le Misanthrope* (1666).

6. Friedrich Schiller, *Love and Intrigue*, in J. G. Fischer, ed., *Schiller's Works*, 4 vols. (Philadelphia: Barrie, 1883), vol. 1, 325.

7. Karl Kraus, *Literatur und Lüge* (Munich: dtv, 1962), 11. (Original hardcover edition published 1958.)

8. Jurek Becker, *Jacob the Liar*, trans. Leila Vennewitz (London: Pan Books, 1990).

9. Psalm 116:11 in the KJV.

10. Augustine of Hippo, *Enchiridion ad Laurentium*, chap. 22;

see Johannes Lindworsky, in Otto Lipmann and Paul Plaut, eds., *Die Lüge in psychologischer, philosophischer, juristischer, pädagogischer, historischer, soziologischer, sprach- und literaturwissenschaftlicher und entwicklungsgeschichtlicher Betrachtung* (Leipzig: Barth, 1927), 56.

11. Thomas Aquinas, *Summa Theologica*, 2.2, question 110 ("Of the Vices Opposed to Truth, and First of Lying"), article 3, in *Summa Theologica*, 3 vols., trans. Fathers of the English Dominican Province (New York: Benziger Brothers, 1947–48), vol. 2, 1666–67; Saint Bonaventure, 3 sent. dist. 38 art. un. qu. 2, ratio 4, cited by Paul Keseling in Saint Augustine, *Die Lüge, und gegen die Lüge*, trans. Paul Keseling (Würzburg: Augustinus, 1953), xxxvii.

12. Dionysius Cato, distich 4.20, *The Distichs of Cato: A Famous Medieval Textbook*, trans. Wayland Johnson Case (Madison: University of Wisconsin, 1922), 39.

13. Voltaire [François-Marie Arouet], "Dialogue Between a Cock and a Hen," in *Micromégas and Other Short Fictions*, trans. Theo Cuffe (New York: Penguin, 2002), 142.

14. Charles Maurice de Talleyrand-Périgord, *Mémoires de Barére*, in Georg Büchmann, comp., *Geflügelte Worte: Der Citatenschatz des deutschen Volkes* (Berlin: Haude und Spenser, 1895), 423.

15. Heinz Friedrich, *Schwierigkeiten, heute die Wahrheit zu schreiben* (Munich: Nymphenburger Verlagshandlung, 1964), 84.

16. Johann Wolfgang von Goethe, *Wilhelm Meister's Apprenticeship*, ed. Nathan Haskell Dole, trans. Thomas Carlyle, 2 vols. (Boston: Francis A. Niccolls, 1901), vol. 2, 78–79; see Leo Spitzer, *Essays in Historical Semantics* (New York: Vanni, 1948), 142.

17. Ludwig Wittgenstein, *Tractatus Logico-Philosophicus*, rev. ed., trans. D. F. Pears and B. F. McGuinness (London: Routledge & Kegan Paul, 1974), 4.002, pp. 35–37.

18. Friedrich Kainz, "Lügenerscheinungen im Sprachleben," in Lipmann and Plaut, eds., *Die Lüge*, 212–43.

19. Saint Augustine, Bishop of Hippo, "Against Lying," chap. 10, para. 24, trans. Harold Jaffee, in *Treatises on Various Subjects*, ed. Roy J. Deferrari (New York: Fathers of the Church, 1952), 152–53.

20. Saint Augustine, Bishop of Hippo, "Lying," chap. 4, para. 4, trans. Mary Sarah Muldowney, in *Treatises*, ed. Deferrari (New York: Fathers of the Church, 1952), 59.

21. Stéphane Mallarmé, "Crisis in Poetry," in *Selected Prose Poems, Essays, and Letters*, trans. Bradford Cook (Baltimore: Johns Hopkins University Press, 1956), 42.

22. Friedrich Nietzsche, "On Truth and Lies in a Nonmoral Sense," in *Philosophy and Truth: Selections from Nietzsche's Notebooks of the Early 1870's*, ed. and trans. Donald Breazeale (Atlantic Highlands, N.J.: Humanities Press, 1979), 85; Leo Weisgerber, *Das Menschheitsgesetz der Sprache als Grundlage der Sprachwissenschaft* (Heidelberg: Quelle and Meyer, 1964), 38–43.

23. Paul Valéry, *Cahiers*, 2, 261; cf. Valéry, *Cahiers*, 5, 825. On Valéry's semantics, see Jürgen Schmidt-Radefeldt, "Semantik und Sprachtheorie in den Cahiers von Paul Valéry" (Ph.D. diss., University of Kiel, 1965). [We have been unable to trace these references to Valéry's notebooks. A number of similar formulations can be readily located, however, in the section "Langage," and in the passages indexed under "Mots et Phrases" and "Phrases," in Paul Valéry, *Cahiers*, ed. Judith Robinson, 2 vols. (Paris: Gallimard, 1973). Examples from vol. 1: "No isolated word has a meaning" (389); "Isolated words are *incomplete*" (438).—Trans.]

24. Ludwig Wittgenstein, *Philosophical Investigations*, trans. G.E.M. Anscombe (New York: Macmillan, 1953), 20e.

25. Peter Hartmann has pointed this out in a different context; see his book *Zur Theorie der Sprachwissenschaft* (Assen: Van Gorcum, 1961), 16–20.

26. Voltaire [François-Marie Arouet], "Languages," in *Voltaire's Philosophical Dictionary*, trans. H. I. Woolf (New York: Knopf, 1924) 178–83; Nathalie Sarraute, *Portrait of a Man Unknown*, trans. Maria Jolas (New York: Braziller, 1958), 66.

27. Jacob and Wilhelm Grimm, "The Devil's Sooty Brother," in *The Complete Fairy Tales of the Brothers Grimm*, trans. Jack Zipes (New York: Bantam, 1987), 367–68.

28. Benedict Spinoza, "Letter L: On Number and Figure in Relation to God," in Spinoza, *Selections*, ed. John Wild (New York: Charles Scribner's Sons, 1930), 454.

29. Marcus Portius Cato, fragment 15, *M. Catonis Praeter Librum de re Rustica Quae Extant*, ed. Heinrich Jordan (Leipzig: Teubner, 1860), 80.

30. Nietzsche, "On Truth and Lies in a Nonmoral Sense," 82.

31. Etienne Bonnot de Condillac, *La langue des calculs: Objet de cet ouvrage*, in *Œuvres philosophiques de Condillac*, ed. Georges Le Roy, 3 vols. (Paris: Presses universitaires de France, 1947–51), vol. 2, 420.

32. For orientation, see, for example, Carl G. Hempel, *Fundamentals of Concept Formation in Empirical Science* (Chicago: University of Chicago Press, 1952). See further Torgny Torgnysson Segerstedt, *Some Notes on Definitions in Empirical Science* (Uppsala: Lundequistska bokhandeln, 1957).

33. Oswald Spengler, *The Decline of the West*, trans. Charles Francis Atkinson, 2 vols. (New York: Knopf, 1922), vol. 2, 144.

34. Johann Wolfgang Goethe, *Faust: Part One*, trans. David Luke (New York: Oxford University Press, 1987), line 2916.

35. Bertolt Brecht, "Writing the Truth: Five Difficulties," trans. Richard Winston, in *Galileo*, ed. Eric Bentley (New York: Grove, 1966), 142.

36. Heinz Friedrich, *Schwierigkeiten heute die Wahrheit zu schreiben: Eine Frage und einundzwanzig Antworten* (Munich: Nymphenburg, 1964), 35.

37. Ibid., 41.

38. Eugen Rosenstock-Huessy, *Die Sprache des Menschenge-schlechts: Eine leibhaftige Grammatik in vier Teilen*, 2 vols. (Heidelberg: Schneider, 1963–64), vol. 2, 116.

39. This is the problem with the disastrously generalized arguments by George Steiner, John McCormick, and Hans Habe about the dehumanization of the German language, reported and discussed in the journal *Sprache im technischen Zeitalter* 6 (May 1963), 431–75. A profitable discussion, however, is found in Victor Klemperer, *The Language of the Third Reich: LTI, Lingua Tertii Imperii: A Philologist's Notebook*, trans. Martin Brady (London: Athlone, 2000). See also Dolf Sternberger, Gerhard Storz, and Wilhelm Emmanuel Süskind, *Aus dem Wörterbuch des Unmenschen* (Hamburg: Classen, 1957).

40. Bertolt Brecht, *The Caucasian Chalk Circle*, in *Seven Plays*, trans. Eric Bentley and Maja Apelman (New York: Grove, 1961), 576 (emphasis added).

41. Augustine, "Lying," chap. 3, para. 3, 55.

42. Augustine, "Against Lying," chap. 10, para. 24, 153.

43. Johann Wolfgang Goethe, *Faust: Part Two*, trans. David Luke (New York: Oxford University Press, 1994), line 7025.

44. I discuss these questions in more detail in the essays "Münze und Wort: Untersuchungen an einem Bildfeld," in Heinrich Lausberg and Harald Weinrich, eds., *Romanica: Festschrift für Gerhard Rohlfs* (Halle: Niemeyer, 1958), 508–21, and "Semantik der kühnen Metapher," *Deutsche Vierteljahrsschrift* 37 (1963), 325–44.

45. Robert Musil, *The Man Without Qualities*, trans. Eithne Wilkins and Ernst Kaiser, 3 vols. to date (London: Pan Books, 1979–), vol. 1, 365.

46. This is discussed in more detail in my book *Tempus: Besprochene und erzählte Welt* (Stuttgart: Kohlhammer, 1964).

47. Hans-Georg Gadamer, "What Is Truth?," trans. Brice R. Wachterhauser, in Brice R. Wachterhauser, ed., *Hermeneutics and Truth* (Evanston: Northwestern University Press, 1994), 33–46.

48. Ibid., 36.

49. Ibid., 43.

50. Augustine, "Against Lying," chap. 3, para. 4, 129.

51. Walther Hofer, ed., *Der Nationalsozialismus: Dokumente 1933–1945* (Frankfurt: Fischer, 1957), 207.

52. Ibid., 204.

53. Søren Kierkegaard, *The Concept of Irony: With Constant Reference to Socrates*, trans. Lee M. Capel (Bloomington: Indiana University Press, 1968), 349; see also the introduction: "It is in Socrates that the concept of irony has its inception in the world" (47).

54. Wolfgang Kayser, *Das sprachliche Kunstwerk* (Berne: Francke, 1962), 111–12.

55. Frédéric Paulhan, *La morale de l'ironie* (Paris: Alcan, 1925), 146.

56. Pierre-Joseph Proudhon, *Les confessions d'un révolution-naire*, in *Œuvres complètes*, ed. Célestin Charles Alfred Bouglé and Henri Moysset, 15 vols. (Paris: Rivière, 1923), vol. 8, 341–42.

57. I follow here a suggestion of Wilhelm Büchner, "Über den Begriff der Eironeia," *Hermes* 76 (1941), 339–58. Goethe uses *Kleintun* in a letter to Zelter dated Feb. 28, 1811; see Johann Wolfgang Goethe, *Werke*, 143 vols. (Weimar: Böhlau, 1887–1919), vol. 22, part 4, 49.

58. Aristotle, *Nicomachean Ethics*, 1127^b25, bk. 4, chap. 7, trans. W. D. Ross, in *Introduction to Aristotle*, ed. Richard McKeon (New York: Random House, 1947), 396.

59. Friedrich Schlegel, "Critical Fragments," trans. Peter Firchow, in David Simpson, ed., *The Origins of Modern Critical Thought: German Aesthetic and Literary Criticism* (Cambridge: Cambridge University Press, 1988), 189.

60. Cicero, *De oratore*, bk. 2, para. 67, 269. [The English translations available to us misrepresent the terminology.]

61. Plato, *Euthyphro*, 5a, trans. Lane Cooper, in *The Collected Dialogues*, ed. Edith Hamilton and Huntington Cairns (New York: Bollingen, 1963), 172.

62. *Euthyphro* 13e, *Dialogues*, 183.

63. Robert Musil, "Aus einem Rapial und andere Aphorismen," in *Tagebücher, Aphorismen, Essays und Reden* (Hamburg: Rowohlt, 1955), 558.

64. Kierkegaard reminds us that Xenophon's Socrates was "irenic" (*irenisk*) rather than ironic; see *The Concept of Irony*, 54, 56.

65. Plato, *Euthyphro*, 14d, *Dialogues* 184.

66. Musil, *Der Mann ohne Eigenschaften* (Hamburg: Rowohlt, 1952), 1603.

67. Carlo Goldoni, The Liar, trans. Grace Lovat Fraser (New York: Knopf, 1922), 22.

68. Jean Cocteau and Georges Feydeau, Thirteen Monologues, trans. Peter Meyer (London: Oberon, 1996), 39.

69. Goldoni, The Liar, 32.

70. Ibid., 60.

71. Pierre Corneille, The Liar, in Seven Plays, trans. Samuel Solomon (New York: Random House, 1969), 444.

72. Lie detectors depend on the (apparently justified) assumption that a lie is always accompanied by lying signals. They move outward in the case of the literary lie, but inward to the psychological circuits of the body in the case of the moral lie. There they can be detected with sensitive instruments. How dependable this procedure is, and whether it is morally justifiable, is a different question.

73. Lucian, Sämtliche Werke, ed. Hans Floerke, 5 vols. (Munich: Georg Müller, 1911), vol. 1, 164. [For an English translation of the dialogue, see Lucian of Samosata, "The Liar," in Works, 4 vols., trans. H. W. Fowler and F. G. Fowler (Oxford: Clarendon Press, 1949), vol. 3, 230–52.]

74. Goldoni, The Liar, 36.

75. See Alexander Rüstow, Der Lügner (Leipzig, 1910).

76. Since antiquity there has also existed a serious, critical variant of this motif. See Ernst Robert Curtius, European Literature and the Latin Middle Ages, trans. Willard R. Trask (New York: Harper and Row, 1963), 94–98.

77. Two nice anthologies of lying literature have appeared recently: Walter Widmer, ed., Lug und Trug: Die schönsten Lügengeschichten der Weltliteratur (Cologne: Kiepenheuer und Witsch,

1963), and Jürgen Dahl, ed., *Reisen nach Nirgendwo: Ein geographisches Lügengarn aus vielerlei fremden Fäden zusammengesponnen* (Düsseldorf: Rauch, 1965). The texts cited are "Das Dithmarsische Lügenmärchen" and "Das erste Lügengedicht," in Widmer, *Lug und Trug*, 302, 296.

78. From Herder's posthumous papers, first published in Wolfgang Kayser, *Die Wahrheit der Dichter: Wandlung eines Begriffs in der deutschen Literatur* (Hamburg: Rowohlt, 1959), 83.

79. Nietzsche, "On Truth and Lies an a Nonmoral Sense," 96 (from Nietzsche's drafts for the essay).

80. Brecht, "Writing the Truth," 135.

Jonah's Sign

It is a true story that Lucian of Samosata and his shipmates got into serious trouble one day. The horrified mariners saw a gigantic whale swimming toward them that was some 1,500 stadia (that is, 150 miles) long. In tears, they bade farewell to one another and to life, and had but a last glimpse of their ship disappearing into the monster's gullet. At once they were engulfed in profound darkness. As their eyes became accustomed to the gloom, however, they realized that their ship had not been dashed to pieces and that they themselves were not dead. Instead, the ship was floating on a lake together with other ships that must have arrived in the fish's belly in the same fashion. A spacious landscape opens up around them, and the sailors leave the ship in order to explore the countryside. They soon encounter other victims of shipwreck, indeed whole peoples who have settled there. They cultivate the land, grow fruit and vines, build temples, inter their dead in graves, and make war on their neighbors. In a word: they live like ordinary human beings. But the war they wage is wretched. The only known weapons are fish bones. How nice that the new arrivals have better weapons at their disposal! They can really help their friends defeat the enemy decisively. But, alas, how little joy derives from such triumphs when you are trapped in the belly of a whale! One must escape! The first attempt, digging a tunnel through the whale's blubber, fails. The second attempt is better planned. The prisoners simply set fire to one of the forests in the fish's belly and burn its body from the inside out. In seven days the beast is dead, and our friends are free. They gratefully sacrifice to Poseidon.

This is a true story, I said, because what I have related can be read in Lucian's *True History*. If I had arbitrarily interrupted this story somewhere in the middle and asked how it continued, it would not have been impossible to guess what might happen next. We all know stories like this, in which someone is swallowed by a whale or some other monster and nevertheless eventually returns in one piece. They are all tall tales. We've read them in the *Facetien* of Heinrich Bebel, the *Wendunmuth* (Cheer Up) of Hans Wilhelm Kirchhof, in the chapbook of the *Lügenhafter Aufschneider* (Lying Rogue), in Abraham a Sancta Clara, or, most likely, in Baron Münchhausen.[1] Bürger's Münchhausen actually has to survive three adventures with a giant fish of this sort. The first of these whales must be about the same size as Lucian's fish. It swallows one ship after another and houses in its belly tens of thousands of people, among them the good baron from Lower Saxony. The second whale is substantially smaller. It measures only half a mile and only drags the lying baron's ship through the sea by its anchor. The third time, the baron encounters a yet smaller animal. It is, to be sure, still big enough to swallow him as he swims near Marseilles, and there probably would have been room for another dozen people, but what's that compared to the territories in the belly of the first whale!

Now let us interrupt our report for a moment and consider in which of the three whale tales the baron of lies has lied the most—the one with the stupendously large, the very large, or the fairly large whale. My position is, the smaller the whale, the bigger the lie. But why? Wouldn't one think that the lie grows in proportion as the tale expands from familiar dimensions to the enormous and immeasurable? Apparently it is just the opposite. The more the lie diverges from normal dimensions, the more harmless the lie. It is not the huge lie but the small, malicious divergence from the truth that is especially dangerous.

Now, it would be a nice thought experiment to let the whales from our stories shrink more and more, and to consider how the story has to change. It is better, however, to look in literature to see how stories are actually told about big fish. In the nineteenth century we meet a real notable among big fish, the white whale Moby Dick, hero of the novel of the same name by Herman Melville. Moby Dick is a very big fish, but he is the right size for a whale. For Herman Melville knows his way around whales; he fills a whole chapter of his novel with a strictly zoological "cetology," a study of whales. The structure of this lovely science remains incomplete, he writes in 1851, rather like the Cologne cathedral with its crane sitting idle atop the half-completed tower. But we don't read the novel today for the sake of this chapter. We admire it rather for the art of the American storyteller, who narrates the great hunt of the whaler Ahab for the white whale Moby Dick so that we can read it also as a parable of the eternal struggle between bold and cunning human activity and the blind, elemental power of nature. Ahab stands "forehead to forehead" with the whale, the small man against the great beast, champions in the primal struggle between dimensions.

Hemingway must have read this novel with great care. His narrative *The Old Man and the Sea* tells again, with different but no less narrative art, the eternal struggle of man with his opponent from the vast. Like the length of the novel, the protagonists have also shrunk. The whale ship is reduced to a fishing boat, and the whale has become a different but still big fish, too big for the weakened arm of the old man. Like Münchhausen's whale, the big fish in Hemingway's story can drag the fisherman's craft behind it through the sea. As in Melville's novel, the merciless struggle ends without triumph. But something else links Melville's novel to Hemingway's story as well. Human and animal are, to be sure, enemies to the death, but they are also mysteriously bound to one another by their hatred, as love does sometimes involve hate.

We have left tall tales far behind us. Or have we? Are the experiences of Melville's whaler and Hemingway's old man the truth? Of course not. Melville's novel is fiction, as is

Hemingway's story. So we have to ask what actually constitutes the difference between tall tales and fiction. Certainly, neither literary genre makes any claim to render true events, and we know that. Only children sometimes fail to realize this and confuse fiction with reality. But gradually they learn. We teach them to recognize the identifying marks of literature, which in the case of certain genres also signal fiction. In individual works, fiction signals are naturally quite variable. We assume, for example, that we have correctly identified Flaubert's *Sentimental Education* as fiction and as a novel, but then are confused by dates and historical occurrences that we recognize from other sources to be nonfictional. Other texts have clearer fiction signals, especially those written for children. Fairy tales are easier to recognize as fiction than historical novels and are, as a result, better training for reading fiction. Among the various signals of fictionality in our literary tradition, one type has lasted because of its striking clarity. It is so clear that we don't even pause to make the observation "This is fiction," but immediately proceed to the next step: "This is a tall tale." That signal, which we have come to know in our stories, is the signal of distorted dimensions. The dimension of the oversized proves these stories fictional, with such convincing clarity, in fact, that, from a certain excessive size on, we inevitably experience this dimension as the dimension of lying.

The same can be said of the dimension of extreme smallness. The difference is primarily that the literature about it does not usually deal in fish. Other animals are preferred: rabbits, mice, guinea pigs, caterpillars, bugs. Alice encounters all of them in Wonderland. Things are such in Wonderland that a drink or a morsel to eat makes Alice sometimes shrink mysteriously to the size of a thumb, sometimes grow into a giant; finally, she no longer knows which way the change will occur: "Which way? Which way?" she asks anxiously. Swift's Gulliver must have felt the same, as his journey made him first a giant in Lilliput, then a dwarf in Brobdingnag. The very large dimension is indeed nothing but the reverse of the very small one, and both kingdoms of lying are interchangeable.

But we shall dwell longer in the very large dimension. We oversimplified there in talking about the truth by omitting Jonah's sign. After all, the prophet Jonah is also swallowed by a great fish (*cetus*). He disobeyed the Lord's command to preach divine vengeance in the heathen city of Nineveh. So he boarded a ship to escape the Lord's call. Then God raises a storm. The sailors are afraid and throw Jonah overboard to protect themselves from God's anger. A whale, as the great fish is generally taken to be, swallows the disobedient prophet and only after three days and three nights does he spit him out again. Jonah's prayers in the whale's belly have soothed God's anger. Now the prophet will perform his assigned task.

Skeptical voices were raised very early on to deny the credibility of the Jonah story. The church fathers, among them Augustine, already had to deal with this kind of biblical criticism.[2] In the course of the centuries, exegetes have made all kinds of efforts to come up with a plausible explanation this side of the supernatural: Jonah was not swallowed by a whale at all but held fast to the back of a (living or dead) fish, or he grabbed a life preserver that was only metaphorically called a whale, or perhaps he just hid in an inn called "The Whale," or else he just dreamed the whole adventure.[3] Recent interpreters don't usually think much of such exegetical feats; instead they point to the mythological background of the Jonah narrative. The tale of a man who is swallowed by a large fish, kills the fish from inside, and returns safely to the light of day seems to be a myth, legend, or fairy tale known all over the world, and indeed with amazing agreement on the details. We have such stories from Portugal, Latvia, Finland, Turkey, Angola, Polynesia.[4] Surely Perseus freeing Andromeda, and Hercules rescuing Hesione from a sea monster, can be counted as members of this—in Melville's phrase— venerable "whaleman's club," which testifies to the "honor and glory of whaling."[5]

Nevertheless, it does not do justice to the biblical tale to reduce it only to the whaling motif and then classify it as mythological. In the Bible and the Christian tradition, the story of the prophet Jonah is handled differently. As the evangelists Matthew and Luke report, when the scholars and pharisees demanded a sign from Christ, he himself reminded them by invoking the tale of Jonah; this evil and perfidious brood wants a sign, but it will receive none other than that of the prophet Jonah. For just as Jonah was in the belly of the great fish for three days and three nights, so will the son of man rest three days and three nights in the womb of the earth.[6] Jonah in the belly of the fish thus points to the crucified Christ, who shall rise again on the third day. An event of the Old Testament and an event of the New Testament are bound together as signs so that the one is the type, *figura*, model, and the other the antitype, *complementum*, fulfillment. The form of thinking expressed here is called *typology*, occasionally also—with less precision—*allegory*.[7] Typology was developed by Paul and the early fathers into a fundamental Christian form of thinking and dominated understanding of the Bible, and, beyond that, the Christian view of history until the modern invention of historicism and its historical-critical methodology. It must be understood that we are dealing with two entirely different conceptions of history and the Christian narrative. Historicism views history, in its chronological sequence, imaged as a river. The older typological method, by contrast, if I may continue the image, builds bridges between two events, first between the Old and New Testaments, then, using the further levels of the fourfold meaning of texts, to the moral life of each Christian, and finally to the expectation for salvation at the eschatological end of time. It must further be understood that the typological way of thinking was not developed by the first Christian theologians as an elegant way to sweep difficulties in biblical interpretation under the rug. Not only does Christ himself, according to the testimony of his evangelists, understand his mission typologically as the fulfillment of the Old Testament, but even the prophets of the Old Testament lay the foundation for typology with their parables. Jonah's

canticle in the belly of the fish is thus not just a lament
on his condition but a typological prayer interpreting that
condition as an image of the most profound depth of
abandonment by God. Jonah understands himself as a
sign. Neither the event of the type (Jonah in the belly of
the fish) nor the event of the antitype (Christ in the womb
of the earth) stands alone; only in their typological cor-
respondence do they constitute a theologically relevant
reality that can be confronted with the question of
whether it is true. This is completely different from tall
tales, but it is also completely different from mythology.
It must be measured by its own standard. So that when
early Christians decorated their graves with the sign of
Jonah, or when Pieter Brueghel draws small fish being
eaten by the next size up but the biggest eater of all being
cut open by the knife of the cross, or when the very fine
Polish poet Zbigniew Herbert addresses "today's Jonah"
in his poem "Jona" as the one not reached by the "bal-
sam of this story,"[8] these all seem to me more appropriate uses of the Jonah story than when someone fusses
around with unnuanced historical criticism and then
must come without fail to the conclusion that the biblical Jonah's whale was not real.

Christian typology dominates broad swaths of European
literature. We know that Dante's *Divine Comedy* is conceived
entirely in terms of typological thinking. It is generally less
well known that Dante also developed a theory of literary
typology in his letter to Can Grande de la Scala and in the
second tractate of the *Convivio*, and with its help sought the

"truth hidden under a beautiful fiction."⁹ Much could be said about this. But instead we shall look at another author of the Romance languages who also accommodated typology, although in a fashion that seems altogether unserious. I mean François Rabelais, who advises his reader in the foreword to *Gargantua* not to believe frivolously that the novel contains nothing but jokes, foolishness, and "gay lies." The reader should rather break open the bones of the book like a shrewd dog and "lick out the substantial marrow"; then he will be the beneficiary of deeper wisdom. Good, let's take his advice and open to chapter 32 of *Pantagruel*. There, Master Alcofribas tells a "most authentic tale."¹⁰ Once, namely when Pantagruel stuck his tongue out—actually, only halfway out—Alcofribas climbed onto this platform and strolled for miles in the enormous mouthscape. There he finds fields and forests, mountains and valleys, cities as big as Lyons and Poitiers, with tens of thousands of inhabitants, who grow cabbage and tend their grapevines. But you have to be careful among what peoples you settle: the ones this side of the Tooth Mountains are decent folk, while on the far side there are only bad people who should be avoided. This makes our narrator start to wonder, since the part of the world in Pantagruel's mouth clearly doesn't differ much from the world of normal dimensions, and since there is lots awry in both.¹¹ "One half of the world doesn't know how the other half lives." Here is the "substantial marrow" lying ready for us. Or should we just take the chapter as a simple lying tale, as a terrestrial variant of the whale stories?

Anyone who reads Pascal will not want to give up the

story's marrow. He will remember the fragment about justice, number 294 in the *Pensées*. What kind of justice is it, Pascal wonders, that can be limited by a mountain range? What is good here is bad there, and vice versa. "Truth this side of the Pyrenees, error on the other!"[12] The word *truth* is striking in this context. Rabelais and Pascal have evidently pondered the same idea, indeed with the same metaphor, and focus on the paradoxes of positive law, which never matches the truth of universal justice. Evidently, this small comparison should show, it is possible to express a profound truth with a tall tale. The truth Pascal wants to express seems in fact to have a special affinity with the literary tradition of distorted dimensions. Let me point to the famous fragment 72, which describes the disproportion of human nature.[13] What is man, Pascal asks, when he seeks to determine his existence in the midst of the vast cosmos? He is nothing in the face of infinity. But the paradox of humankind is only half comprehended when its disproportion to vastness is considered. The opposite train of thought leads to the same oppressive result. What is man, considered in comparison to what is extremely small? Something very tiny—a mite, say—is just as inaccessible to human thought as something gigantic.[14] Human reason gets lost in infinity in both directions. Humanity stands helpless between the infinitely large and the infinitely small, "a middle term between nothing and all."[15] And Pascal drives the refractory human spirit now toward the large dimension, now toward the small, until he realizes "that he is an incomprehensible monster."[16]

It is surely no accident that Pascal in the *Pensées* forces the human mind into the two dimensions of the very large and the very small, familiar to us from the tall tales of many different times. He is evidently concerned with a truth that cannot be entrusted to plain declarative sentences, but must rather be experienced through shock. For this he makes use of the alienation in size otherwise reserved to the tall tale. Here also, truth and lying seem closer together than they would appear at first glance. Those familiar with French literature will be surprised, on reading this and other fragments of Pascal, to find mites and monsters discussed in so serious a text. Such things are otherwise not to be found in classical French literature. The sea monster ("monstre marin") that swallows Hippolyte at the end of Racine's tragedy *Phaedra* is the sole exception. But of course the brute never appears onstage; it is present only through the messenger speech of Theramenes. It is very revealing that Leo Spitzer, one of the great masters of literary interpretation, once explicated *Phaedra* entirely on the basis of this messenger's speech and came to the conclusion that the play conceals a baroque Racine behind the classical Racine.[17] The Baroque has other dimensions, nonclassical ones.

Nevertheless, the literature of French classicism, like other European national literatures before and after it, submitted to the rules of Aristotelian poetics and adopted the strict rule of verisimilitude. To be sure, fiction is not required to conform to actual circumstances, as historiography is, but its range is narrowed by the limits of what is possible. But what is understood to be possible and probable is, at bottom, what belongs to our dimension. Of course, there remains a difference in dimension between the high genre of tragedy and the low genre of comedy, but that is only a difference in the height of the cothurnus. Since the age of classicism, the very large and the very small have been excluded from canonical literature and driven to the margins. In fairy tales, fables, children's stories, and, admittedly, tall tales, there can still be giants and dwarves and the grotesque transformative play of dimensions: official poetics has no interest in them. It acknowledges no literature beyond the pale of verisimilitude.

As a result, all literature is now divided—I am simplifying—into three parts. In the middle is the verisimilar literature in the spirit of Aristotle's poetics. To one side, we find historiography as the literature of truth; on the other, tall tales as the literature of untruth. Is it any wonder, under these circumstances, that tall tales model themselves more on the literature of truth than on the literature of verisimilitude? They claim to be "true stories" and assert their truthfulness (not their probability) as their most common lying signal. That is doubtless, as Schiller would say, "the brazen confidence of lying."

Modern literature is no longer Aristotelian in the strict sense. Indeed, among some recent authors it is distinctly un-Aristotelian. If we examine this observation with respect to the dimensions of large and small, we will initially find that the literature of our century generally sticks to the moderate dimension of verisimilitude. People on our scale are the protagonists of modern novels and dramas, and literature tends more and more to reduce even the moral excess, the severe ethos of a Corneille, for example, or the far-reaching enthusiasm of a Schiller to the smaller measure of the everyday. Realism and naturalism push this reduction even further and seek increasingly to express the ordinary. These are all variations within verisimilitude, of course, with the tendency to make probability ever more unmistakably like truth by adopting scientific methods of observation and experimentation. Literature seems to be trying to move yet further from the zone of untruth.

But we shouldn't have unreserved faith in the manifestos and declarations. To be sure, Julien Sorel, the good soldier Schwejk, and Raskolnikov don't get swallowed by whales, but are they really wrecked by powers of their own dimension? Emile Zola wrote a novel in which everything happens very realistically and naturalistically. It is about a man named Florent who works as an inspector in the Paris markets. His daily life amid the working rhythm of the markets is described with such precision that we are aware the author studied this world scientifically. The description is exact, down to the innumerable varieties of cheese in the famous "cheese symphony." But, if I can ask the patient reader to linger over it for a moment, it is striking how strongly the style is marked by expressions of enormity and hugeness. Mountains pile up, summits tower, bellies swell. This is in fact a stylistic constant of the whole novel. The markets of Paris are indeed minutely observed and exactly described, yet the style of description is not neutral but consistently shifts the dimension of the objects represented into the dimension of the oversized, the huge. The market halls are titanic, enormous, gigantic, massive, colossal, monstrous; they resemble an entire city or the wide sea. They also resemble, and this is the central metaphor of the novel *The Belly of Paris* (1873), a huge belly, the belly of the beast that is Paris. Man—the hero Florent, if one can still speak about heroes—is trapped in this belly, and the story leads him to the point at which, with profound terror, he recognizes his imprisonment. From this imprisonment there is no escape, and it presses in on him like a fresh nightmare every night.[18]

I think we may cautiously generalize on these observations. The realistic and naturalistic styles often do not stop with the precise registration of actual conditions and social relations. They go beyond that and maneuver their characters into the position of smallness vis-à-vis their conditions and social relations so that everything crashes down upon them. The characters and their environments are of different dimensions and are archenemies.

From this point of view, even the most recent literature, with its tendency to paradox, demonism, and absurdity, is not a rejection of realism and naturalism but their continuation and further development. The dimensions once suppressed by Aristotelianism are returning in force to high literature. Thus Franz Kafka turns the hero of his story "Die Verwandlung" ("The Metamorphosis," 1916) into a "giant insect." Julien Green calls a novel *Léviathan* (1929).[19] Ionesco has more and more furniture delivered to a new tenant until he disappears behind the mountain of furniture (*The New Tenant*, 1957). Henri Michaux sings of his rage as a lyric poet, and that is the very small dimension, and in his rage is an egg, and in the egg are his mother, his father, and his children ("Je suis gong," "I am going"). In a different poem, "Tu Viendras" he invokes an Other from the very large dimension:

TU VIENDRAS,

Tu viendras, si tu existes,
appâté par mon gâchis,
mon odieuse autonomie;
Sortant de l'éther, de n'importe où,
    de dessous mon moi bouleversé, peut-être;
jetant mon allumette dans Ta démesure,
et adieu, Michaux . . . [20]

YOU WILL COME

you will come, if you exist,
baited by my mire,
my odious autonomy;
Bursting from the Ether, from somewhere or other,
    from under my overturned self, maybe;
hurling my match into Your boundlessness,
and goodbye, Michaux . . . [21]

In conclusion, let me mention from recent German literature Martin Walser's *Lügengeschichten* (Lying Tales, 1964) so that the connection with tall tales becomes visible one last time. The first of these tall tales is called "My Giant Problem." It begins: "I, yes, I, am selling my giant." The point of the story, of course, is that the narrator cannot get rid of his giant, which he also calls his "worry whale." That is the problem with giants. Apparently none of us can get rid of our giants.

NOTES

1. Heinrich Bebel, "Liber tertius 13: De quodam sacerdote carnifice," *Heinrich Bebels Facetien drei Bücher,* ed. Gustav Bebermeyer (Leipzig: Hiersemann, 1931), 110–11. See also Hans Wilhelm Kirchhof, *Wendunmuth,* 5 vols., ed. Hermann Oesterley (Tübingen: Litterarischer Verein in Stuttgart, 1868), vol. 4; Hans Wilhelm Kirchhof, *Das Schaltjahr,* 5 vols., ed. J. Scheible (Stuttgart: Verlag des Herausgebers, 1846–47), vol. 1, 499, and vol. 4, 122. See further Abraham a Sancta Clara, *Wunderwürdiges gantz neu ausgeheck-tes Narren-Nest: Sämtliche Werke,* 17 vols. (Passau: 1840), vol. 13, 28, in Karl Müller-Fraureuth, *Die deutschen Lügendichtungen bis auf Münchhausen* (Halle: 1881; Hildesheim: Olms, 1965), 48.

2. See the evidence in Peter Friedrichsen, *Kritische Übersicht der verschiedenen Ansichten von dem Buche Jonas* (Leipzig: 1845), 1n1.

3. Friedrichsen, *Kritische Übersicht,* 25, 28, 69–70, 292. Cf. Herman Melville, *Moby Dick,* ed. Harrison Hayford, Hershel Parker, and G. Thomas Tanselle, chap. 83 ("Jonah Historically Regarded") (Evanston: Northwestern University Press, 1988), 364–66.

4. See Ludwig Radermacher, "Walfischmythen," *Archiv für Religionswissenschaft* 9 (1906), 248–52. For general documentation, see also Antti Amatus Aarne, *The Types of the Folktale: A Classification and Bibliography,* trans. Stith Thompson (Helsinki: Suomalainen Tiedeakatemia, 1961). See also Stith Thompson, *Motif-Index of Folk Literature,* 6 vols. (Bloomington: Indiana University Press, 1955–58).

5. Melville, *Moby Dick*, chap. 82 ("The Honor and Glory of Whaling"), in *The Writings of Herman Melville*, vol. 6, 363–64.

6. Matthew 12:39–40. Cf. Matthew 16:4 and Luke 11:29–30.

7. On typology, see Erich Auerbach, "Figura," trans. Ralph Manheim, in *Scenes from the Drama of European Literature* (New York: Meridian, 1959), 11–76. See also Erich Auerbach, *Typologische Motive in der mittelalterlichen Literatur* (Krefeld: Scherpe, 1953); Henri de Lubac, *Histoire et esprit: L'intelligence de l'Ecriture d'après Origène* (Paris: Aubier, 1950); Henri de Lubac, *Medieval Exegesis*, trans. Mark Sebanc (Grand Rapids, Mich.: W. B. Eerdmans, 1998).

8. Herbert Zbigniew, *Gedichte*, trans. Karl Dedecius (Frankfurt: Suhrkamp, 1964), 33.

9. Dante Alighieri, "To Can Grande Della Scala," in *The Letters of Dante*, trans. Paget Toynbee (Oxford: Clarendon, 1920), 73; Dante Alighieri, *Convivio*, trans. William Walrond Jackson (Oxford: Clarendon, 1909), 67–119.

10. François Rabelais, *Gargantua and Pantagruel*, trans. J. M. Cohen (Harmondsworth: Penguin, 1974), 38, 273.

11. Erich Auerbach, "The World in Pantagruel's Mouth," in *Mimesis: The Representation of Reality in Western Literature*, trans. Willard R. Trask (Princeton: Princeton University Press, 1953), 262–84.

12. Blaise Pascal, fragment 108 [294 in French], *Pensées*, trans. Martin Turnell (London: Harvill Press, 1962), 139–41.

13. See Michel Philip, "L'idée d'infini dans les 'Pensées' de Pascal," *Revue des sciences humaines* 111 (July–Sept. 1963), 295–303.

14. Whales and mites are also the representatives of the very large and very small dimensions in Jean de la Fontaine, "The Double Sack," fable 1.7 in *The Complete Fables of Jean de la Fontaine*,

trans. Norman B. Spector (Evanston: Northwestern University Press, 1988), 13–15.

15. Pascal, fragment 390 [72], *Pensées*, 214–21.

16. Pascal, fragment 245 [420], ibid., 167.

17. Leo Spitzer, "The Récit de Théramène," *Linguistics and Literary History* (Princeton: Princeton University Press, 1948), 87–134.

18. In the words of Lukács, "In Balzac's writings social forces never appear as romantic and fantastic monsters (as, e.g., later in Zola)"; see Georg Lukács, *Studies in European Realism* (New York: Grosset and Dunlap, 1964), 41. On the social transformation of the myth, see also Bertolt Brecht's prose piece "If Sharks Were Men" in *Stories of Mr. Keuner*, trans. Martin Chambers (San Francisco: City Lights, 2001), 45.

19. See Julien Green, *The Dark Journey*, trans. Vyvyan Holland (New York: Harper and Brothers, 1929).

20. Henri Michaux, "Mais toi, quand viendras-tu," in *Plume, précédée de Lointain intérieur* (Paris: Gallimard, 1938). The poem "Je suis gong" is from the collection *Mes propriétés* (Paris: Fourcade, 1929).

21. Henri Michaux, "You There, When Are You Coming?," in *Selected Writings: The Space Within*, trans. Richard Ellmann (New York: New Directions, 1944), 229.

Politeness, an Affair of Honor

Honor is one thing, politeness another, of course, but it may be worth considering whether and how these two values—if they are values—belong together, both by their very nature and especially by their historical connection. I will explore this question in a three-step argument. In the first step, I present historical material for consideration in three literary examples; they are Tirso de Molina's Don Juan, Goethe's *Faust*, and the Bishop of Verona according to Giovanni Della Casa. In the second step, I use these examples to compare the code of honor and the code of politeness in their classical literary manifestations. As a third and final step, I consider what survives of these codes of behavior today and may remain valid tomorrow.

When the Spanish Mercedian monk Gabriel Téllez, known as Tirso de Molina, wrote *El burlador de Sevilla*, in 1620, he created in the protagonist of his play, Don Juan, the hero of a modern myth.[1] In this myth the "power of fate" is tied to honor. The hero, Don Juan Tenorio, is a man of honor. This is his view of himself, and it is the view of his society. By nature, however, he is a born seducer, and he knows it:

> El mayor
> gusto que en mí puede haber
> es burlar una mujer
> y dejalla sin honor.

> My very favourite pastime, my delight's
> To trick a woman, steal away her honour,
> Deprive her of her treasured reputation.[2]

We see that Don Juan finds no problem for his honor when he seduces and dishonors women, married or unmarried: by his lights, the honor of men and that of women are two different things.

How many women does this artist of seduction seduce? Is it really, as Leporello calculates in Mozart/Da Ponte's *Don Giovanni*, one thousand and three in Spain alone? In Tirso it is "only" four. I shall choose one case from this catalogue of seductions: Tisbea.

On his flight from Italy, where he has seduced a Neapolitan princess, Don Juan is caught in a storm at sea and is wrecked on the Spanish coast. Tisbea, a fisherman's daughter, kindly takes him into her hut and offers him hospitality. Hospitality to strangers is the oldest and perhaps most noble form of politeness.[3] Homer's Odysseus, as shipwrecked stranger with Nausicaa, is probably the literary model for this scene.[4] But unlike Homer, whose hero respects the rights and duties of guests, Don Juan shamelessly exploits the privilege of staying the night in his hostess's hut to seduce the innocent girl and then to abandon her.

The dialogue that leads up to this seduction is characterized by an entirely different kind of politeness, namely, by "courtesy" as it was established in the Middle Ages as a cultural code.[5] Don Juan addresses the fisherman's daughter as "Lady" ("señora"); her lovely locks have ensnared his soul, her radiant eye has pierced his heart, and the lover will die if the beloved does not instantly hear his plea. And lest she think that the honor of his class might be a hindrance, she may be informed "Amor es rey": love is sovereign and ranks above honor. This is actually not the case, as the man of honor Don Juan well knows; instead, honor stands as the highest value, above all other public and private values, even above life, and of course above love.[6] Don Juan uses the language of polite gallantry—of which, as a man of honor, he is a complete master—solely as an instrument of seduction against a fisherman's daughter, who still takes these metaphors at face value and believes the gallant's oaths.

For my second example I have chosen Goethe's *Faust*: the Gretchen episode, which constitutes a bourgeois tragedy and belongs to the classical literature of honor.[7] The middle-class Margarete knows well what her respectability requires:

Sie ist so sitt-und tugendreich,
Und etwas schnippisch doch zugleich.

So virtuous, so decent, yet
A touch of sauciness as well![8]

She has to be a touch saucy, in order—in politely coquettish fashion—to be able to keep overeager men in their place. That is part and parcel of her role in this kind of politeness and is also the way she responds to Faust's approach when he accosts her on her way home from church. The lines are well known:

Faust
Mein schönes Fräulein, darf ich wagen,
Meinen Arm und Geleit Ihr anzutragen?

Margarete
Bin weder Fräulein, weder schön,
Kann ungeleitet nach Hause gehn.

Sie macht sich los und geht ab.

Faust
My sweet young lady, if I may
I will escort you on your way.

Margarete
I'm not a lady and I'm not sweet,
I can get home on my own two feet.

She frees herself and walks on.[9]

The final stage direction reveals that Faust rapidly becomes rather abrupt and immediately takes hold of the arm he asks for in such polite, indeed overly polite, language so that Margarete, at least at first, has to shake him off. Her hostile language is appropriate for a bourgeois young mistress (this is her view of herself) "saucily" rejecting the inappropriate aristocratic address "Fräulein," the empty compliment, and finally the improper offer to accompany her in public. She knows what to expect from this kind of exaggerated politeness, and she is of course entirely clear, even here with the first exchange, that her womanly honor is at stake. For the site of honor is always the public sphere.

Faust is not deterred, however, and the seduction proceeds, minus polite detours, since Faust is carried away by his raging passion and has little patience for the "indirect manner," as Goethe once defined politeness.[10] In these scenes, Mephistopheles, whom Madame de Staël styles a "civilized devil," behaves much better than Faust, whose outspokenness tends to boorishness, especially toward Mephistopheles.[11] So Faust must learn better manners, from Margarete herself, who describes Faust's behavior in the encounter scene as follows:

> Es schien ihm gleich nur anzuwandeln,
> Mit dieser Dirne g'rade hin zu handeln.

> He suddenly just thinks, quite without shame:
> "I'll pick this girl up."[12]

To be sure, "Dirne" did not then mean "whore," as it does now, but there is distinct condemnation of Faust in the expression "gerade hin," which identifies the exact opposite of the "indirect manner." Margarete has thus confidently understood Faust's excessive politeness as rudeness, with complete justification. But Faust already understands that he owes the young woman an apology:

> Und du verzeihst die Freiheit, die ich nahm,
> Was sich die Frechheit unterfangen,
> Als du jüngst aus dem Dom gegangen?

> And you've forgiven the liberty
> I took outside the church, the insulting way
> I spoke to you the other day?[13]

This small victory on the terrain of manners doesn't help Maid Margarete for very long. Like Don Juan's Tisbea, she will soon be seduced and abandoned by her lover, a victim of honor. Was she perhaps not saucy enough?

My third example is entirely different. I take it from a treatise on manners published by the Italian archbishop and papal nuncio Giovanni Della Casa in 1558, under the title *Galateo*.[14] This "tractate of social rhetoric"[15] was an unparalleled best-seller in Italy (and soon after in Spain as well) so that even today Italians say of someone with poor manners, "He doesn't know his *Galateo*."

In the fourth chapter of this work there is an anecdote that Alain Pons calls the heart of this textbook of politeness. The author is talking about a visit paid by Count Ricciardo to the Bishop of Verona. They spend a few days together conversing pleasantly; these are holidays in the courtly-courteous custom. Now the guest is about to leave. The bishop considers with his household whether he might call the attention of this guest, who has displayed such superb manners during his visit, to "one small fault" ("un picciolo difetto") so that his manners will henceforth be perfect. What is the count's problem? He smacks his lips when he eats. This is what the bishop wants to make him realize, but as cautiously and gently as can be imagined. So he asks a good friend named Galateo (whence the title of the work) to accompany the departing guest for the first day of his journey and to impart to him, as much in passing as possible, and as the explicit parting gift of the bishop, the gently reproving hint ("la sua amorevole reprensione ed avvertimento") that at table the count's "chewing makes a strange sound which is unpleasant to hear."[16] The count reddens slightly but quickly controls himself and parts from his hosts with genuine thanks.

This third story, as I have wanted to show, represents a viewpoint quite different from the first two, summarized from the dramas of honor *El Burlador de Sevilla* and *Faust*. These were clearly narratives of falls; the third event is, by contrast, an exemplum. So differently indeed do honor and good manners appear in literature. Classical European literature, with its high point in the seventeenth and eighteenth centuries, is a highly developed casuistics of honor.

As a result, there is a distinct preference for those literary genres that think in terms of cases. This means first drama (tragedy, comedy, bourgeois tragedy), such as we have seen with Tirso de Molina and Goethe. The novella is also preferred, since its short form naturally suits it to casuistic representation. Its earliest masters are Boccaccio and Cervantes. In these dramas and novellas, the most interesting cases involving honor are played out—tragically, comically, ambivalently, but always sharply profiled—with special emphasis on borderline and problematic cases in which the code of honor seems especially in need of clarification. The two dramas presented above about Don Juan and Faust are of this sort.

For the code of politeness, other literary genres are primary, especially the novel and other forms of social prose. Often they are collections of aphorisms, as with Gracián, La Rochefoucauld, and Schopenhauer, but there are also works that are basically like treatises except that they present their lessons not with dry pedantry but in a pleasant, conversational style. Texts in these genres present, however, not cases but examples in which good and bad manners can be demonstrated. Characteristic examples of these genres in the Romance literatures would be Honoré d'Urfé's novel *Astrée* and the above-mentioned work *Galateo*, by Giovanni Della Casa. But this treatise is only one of many in a long and brilliant tradition that includes Castiglione's *Courtesan*, Gracián's *Oracle*, La Bruyère's *Characters*, Lord Chesterfield's *Letters to his Son*, and of course Knigge's tract *The Art of Conversing with Men*, and in a certain sense also the somewhat drier Latin treatise *The Civility of Child-hood*, by the humanist Erasmus of Rotterdam, a treatise that became a much read textbook of manners for all of Europe. In all these texts, honor and politeness interact in complex ways.

Giovanni Della Casa thought with particular success about how this works. At the beginning of his *Galateo* he defends himself against the conceivable reproach that politeness might seem really frivolous ("frivolo") in comparison to other learning required by a man of honor. Naturally, he admits, bravery ("fortezza") and greatness of soul ("grandezza dell' animo") are higher values or, in his words, more noble virtues—but how seldom is there opportunity or need for demonstrating them. Good manners, however, are necessary every day; their frequent use compensates for their relatively low rank in the canon of virtues. Considered from the standpoint of vices, the circumstances are even clearer. Violations of the major virtues, according to Della Casa, are to be feared like wild beasts ("fiere salvatiche"), but, fortunately, they are rarely encountered. But the numerous tiny violations of good manners to which one is exposed daily are as annoying and bothersome as mosquitoes and horseflies ("zanzare e mosche"), and this constant irritation can easily develop into significant discomfort.

Thus we find in Della Casa a distinction between major and minor morality, described with penetrating imagery and linked to the welcome tendency to give higher moral value to the "small change" of daily politeness (as Kant calls it) or the "minima moralia" (Adorno's term), compared to the heroic virtues associated with the acme of honor.[17]

Are honor and politeness virtues at all in the classical sense of the word? In the canon of the four cardinal virtues—wisdom, justice, courage, temperance—honor does not appear but is close to courage. Honor is fundamentally different, however, because it represents no ethical value in and of itself but expresses the high opinion held by *others* (to the extent that they themselves are possessed of honor) of the absolute value of the honorable man's personal worth. This of course requires him to be constantly prepared to challenge with drawn blade every publicly expressed doubt of his worth, even at the cost of his own life. To that extent, the waxing and waning of honor is given over to the social milieu and the public sphere.

There is, in this respect, a certain though limited analogy to the long catalogue of manners that constitutes the code of politeness. The paradigm of polite social intercourse for all the great guides to politeness, from Castiglione to Knigge, is to accommodate *others*, to be as pleasant as possible to them so as actually to please them. In this fashion the sharp corners and hard edges of human social life are to be smoothed as much as possible. This leads to a broad range of social behaviors that extend, in Della Casa, to return once more to the Bishop of Verona, from avoiding smacking the lips while eating to the very gently administered criticism of such misconduct. And above all there must never be any appearance of difficulty or effort. For ease ("sprezzatura"), according to Castiglione and many other guides, is the very first commandment of good manners.[18]

By now both history and literature have perhaps done their part to consolidate our impression of what is to be understood by semiotics as a code of honor and politeness. It clearly does not mean an articulated theoretical system but rather a set or even a catalogue of linguistic signs and norms that in any given epoch guide the cultural conduct of a social group and thus also guarantee its cohesiveness. The code of honor has unquestionably a more rigid structure: there is no gray area between honor and disgrace. There is only yes or no, which can always also mean life or death when honor comes into question. This harsh alternative underlies the aristocracy's existence as the caste of honor.

What is its relationship to the code of politeness, which, by contrast, consists entirely of subtleties and nuances? This question forms the starting point for the remarkable investigations into the historical interplay of honor and politeness by Claude Chauchadis, a "politessologiste" (a term occasionally used in France).[19] Using a generic reference widespread in French advice books, the author argues that politeness ("politesse") means "knowing how to live" ("savoir vivre"), while honor often leads to the opposite, "knowing how to die" ("savoir mourir").[20] How do they fit together? Chauchadis answers with a pragmatic moral argument. In his view it must be in the interest of the man of honor to find a respectable way to keep the extreme life-or-death case from arising at every trivial provocation. There has to be a social strategy of avoidance to prevent insult and loss of honor in the first place. This, according to Chauchadis, is the special task of politeness, which may therefore be characterized as a strategy of avoidance and in this sense as "negative politeness." It is no surprise, he concludes, that Spain, where the code of honor ("pundonor") reached its sharpest expression, also produced the most ceremonious forms of etiquette and a rather cold-blooded, strategic politeness that combines shrewdness and diplomatic caution in the concept *discreción*. Baltasar Gracián is its theoretician.[21]

I would like to try to clarify this in three further comparisons. First, the question will be how the two sexes are seen in the two codes, that of honor and that of politeness. It turns out that the honor code tends to be masculine, the politeness code feminine. At the center of the honor code is masculine honor, which must be defended with weapon in hand against every insult. Its liturgy is the duel, as can be learned from many dramas of honor (so that using a sword belongs to the regular training of actors to this day). Women's honor, which differs in many respects from men's, depends in the last analysis upon it, since a woman who loses her virginity or a woman who violates the commandment of faithfulness in marriage brings more disgrace to the male members of her family than to herself—which may be understood tragically or comically, depending on the genre. To that extent, by the rules of this code, feminine honor is only a pendant to masculine honor.

The reverse is true with regard to gender and politeness, which in Europe since the high Middle Ages has taken a different course from the corresponding codes in other cultures; more precisely: since the troubadours, politeness has taken a specifically feminine turn, in the form of courtesy. The founding act of this polite gallantry is the invention of the lady, an artificial figure around whom almost all European politeness is organized, with far-reaching consequences for all literature and culture. At the center of this conduct stands the conversation, a gay and witty form of linguistic intercourse, the rules of which are determined predominantly according to the pleasure or displeasure of the ladies. In this respect, the two codes complement one another.

This is also revealed by a second peculiarity of the two codes in question. It was once common to say of a man who lacked honorability that he had no "honor in his body." The characterization is correct insofar as honor, in the terms of the honor code, is in fact located in the body, indeed primarily in the heart, in the blood, and in the arm with the hand that wields the sword. Everything that attacks honor touches the body, and in this sense "touches on honor," like a slap in the face but also an insulting word that makes the face redden with anger, and correspondingly all affairs of honor ultimately concern "body and soul." The same is true for women's honor, which is also located in the body, in the reproductive organs, which transmit to the next generation, by blood, the claim to honor. The rigid consistency of the honor code through centuries of European history depends in essence on this fundamental corporeality.

It is not possible to say the same about the code of politeness without qualification. Yet this code also has strong corporeal components to the extent that its rules not only impose the wittiest possible use of language but also demand firm control of the polite person's creatureliness. Avoiding lip-smacking at table is part of it. For Erasmus, who writes for teachers and pupils, that is the most important aspect of *civilitas*.[22] Meeting these conditions requires control of gestures, movements, and all nonverbal behavior. In social intercourse it is not enough to avoid offenses through one's physical presence, but one must also make the most graceful and elegant possible use of it. The French aphorist Alain, to whom we owe a series of interesting observations on manners in our century, liked to compare good manners with dancing and surely touched on something essential with this characterization.[23] Hence we often speak of "tact"[24] when politeness is meant.

The two codes of behavior can be compared in yet a third respect. In many dramas of honor, as, for example, in Corneille's *The Cid*, we see a tragic conflict of honor, which in fact admits of no peaceful resolution, solved through the intervention of the king. He can resolve conflicts because he differs from everyone else of honorable rank in that he not only possesses honor but is honor itself. All honor in society proceeds from him as the *fons honorum* and returns at last to him, who only "confers" it. In this respect, the sovereign constitutes the center of the honor code, and everything related to honor revolves about this sun—in France, the Sun King.

Even that can be said only in comparable but not identical form about politeness. It does not proceed directly from the sovereign but does have its distinct "source." That is the court, which gives its name to courtesy in English and French and to politeness in German (*Höflichkeit*, from *Hof*, court). It is of course the court of a sovereign, like that of the Duke of Urbino in Castiglione's *Cortegiano*; nevertheless, the focus of behavior relevant to politeness is on the courtiers, ladies and gentlemen, and not actually the ruler. Just as the court surrounds the ruler, it can be said in general that the code of politeness forms a ring and semiotic field around the inner code of honor so that its harsh pathos is veiled and softened by the gentler ethos of politeness. This does, to be sure, offer opportunities to predatory and gambling natures, like the great seducers, to steal into the secret heart of honor under the cloak of politeness, and in this way, as we say these days, to break the code.

What happens now to honor and politeness in the nineteenth and twentieth centuries? It may be said for both codes, first of all, that they basically maintain their allure in parallel, indeed extend it and spread to the high bourgeoisie. "What a Man Represents": in this phrase from Schopenhauer's *Aphorismen zur Lebensweisheit*, bourgeois honor and bourgeois politeness amicably join.[25] But how firmly established is this normative order? I shall not attempt to answer this question sociologically but only call attention to two earthquakes that shook to its foundations the building in which honor and politeness set up housekeeping together. (In concrete terms, one might think of Thomas Mann's patrician Buddenbrook dynasty.) Both tremors began before the Enlightenment. The propagation of equality in the historical context of the French Revolution unhinged traditional honor, and, with the invention of sincerity, something similar happened to the old politeness, above all in the works of Rousseau.[26] Both cultural heritages, honor and politeness, have belonged since then not exactly to the rubbish heap but to the ancien régime. I shall elaborate, using two French authors: Alexis de Tocqueville has drawn up the account of honor, Germaine de Staël that of politeness.

Alexis de Tocqueville engages the problematics of honor in *Democracy in America* (1835–40). Beginning from Montesquieu's tripartite typology of political forms and their three driving forces, he distinguishes despotism (driven by fear), republic (driven by civic virtue), and monarchy (driven by honor). In his view, the French monarchy, reestablished after the Revolution, is kept going by the dynamics of aristocratic honor, even though this is, as he immediately concedes, an essentially irrational, a "bizarre" and "capricious," driving force. But his actual theme is America, more precisely, the democratic republican political structure of the United States. He determines what could already have been postulated from

Montesquieu, that in the New World a modern political system can evidently manage—almost—without honor. To be sure, Tocqueville finds relics of honor here and there in American society, but it is now a religion in which no one any longer believes, and its temples have been abandoned. America is driven instead by the powers of work and money, combined of course with civic virtue, as Montesquieu had also foretold. And, lo and behold, it works even without honor! Tocqueville derives from this the prognosis, "It is the dissimilarities and inequalities among men which give rise to the notion of honor; as such differences become less, it grows feeble; and when they disappear, it will vanish too."[27]

For similar thoughts on the problem of politeness, we must go back a few decades to find Germaine de Staël as the author of *On Literature Considered in Its Relationship to Social Institutions*. Part 2, chapter 2, concerns us especially: "On Taste and Civilized Manners, and Their Literary and Political Influence."[28] Madame de Staël bases her reflections on the French Revolution as a historical fact and on the basic human right of equality as a political given. She respects republican sensibilities by calling politeness "refinement of manners," for she has no desire to return to the "exaggerated delicacies" of prerevolutionary codes of behavior.[29] Yet she is appalled by the "revolting vulgarity of manners" that has appeared in the recent revolutionary period.[30] Society must find its way from these bad habits back to "good taste," and that is, for Madame de Staël, not just a literary or cultural question but a political one.

In her view, accordingly, what is necessary is "education for liberty," through which the material work of the Revolution can be completed spiritually.[31] A new politeness must be sought, whose goal she defines as follows: "Perfect manners encourage whatever is distinguished in every person, inhibiting nothing but his faults."[32] That is truly a new kind of politeness, compared to that of the ancien régime; Madame de Staël also calls it "dignity of manners," and it approaches what recent scholarship on politeness identifies as "positive politeness." Far removed from "negative politeness," with its anxious avoidance strategies, this can be defined as a social stance that takes interest in what is different in other people and then attempts to see in the differences qualities that deserve to be acknowledged with approbation.[33] This positive politeness is not only "a sort of equality in inequality," as Madame de Staël said elsewhere about the old politeness (*Germany*, part 1, chap. 11; 1:85), but can better be called, conversely, an inequality in equality, whose openness to differentiation makes equality bearable at all.

With these ideas in mind, we can now consider, in conclusion, whether honor and politeness can still lay any claim to validity, once there is no longer any generally accepted code for either form of behavior. Is it perhaps even possible that the *disiecta membra* of the one code and the other could be reconstituted into a new, common code?

If that were to be conceivable, then first and foremost equality would have to be made real, since it can no longer be rescinded. This principle appears the most consistently

in the catalogue of basic rights that has become a regular constituent of democratic constitutions since the
American Declaration of Independence and the French
Revolution. In this catalogue, human dignity might then
occupy the place that honor held under conditions of
inequality.[34] Human dignity could thus identify the center of an integrated code of behavior that we might name,
by borrowing from Erasmus of Rotterdam and Norbert
Elias, a code of civility. Here one could bring together
those elements of old codes of honor and politeness that
do not conflict with the principle of equality and are
therefore worth saving.

In order to prevent sterile leveling, however, it is equally
important to include, in a highly visible section of such a
code of civility, the above-mentioned positive politeness,
which not only seeks in others what connects to all other
people but also sympathetically searches out in individual
otherness the interesting differences that constitute their
valuable uniqueness and perhaps their entire personal
distinction. There, some of the qualities of the old honor
are preserved as well.

This simultaneously honorable and polite virtue of
civility is especially called for now, when the differentness
of other people is striking, when, for example, foreigners
live among us who have special difficulties orienting themselves to our environment and as a result require special
attentiveness, kindness, and assistance. To be sure, it is now
no longer possible, it seems to me, to return without further
reflection to one of the oldest and most venerable forms

of civility, the ancient sanctity of the guest and the principle of courteous and generous hospitality that depends upon it. There is too much motion and unrest in our modern world for the role of the stranger, once surrounded by special politeness, not to be negatively affected.

Even so, I think we should consider placing the figure of the stranger at the center of a new code of civility and measuring this humanitarian norm of behavior by how much honor is shown to strangers, or, one could say, how much positive politeness is accorded precisely to otherness.

But the stranger is not only the man or woman with a different passport; all those are strangers who, in the language of Walter Benjamin, are called underdogs. Of them Benjamin writes, in a reflection written in 1932, that politeness is most dependably recognized by its readiness to offer "a real chance for the underdog."[35]

NOTES

1. Tirso de Molina, El burlador de Sevilla, in Comedias, ed. Américo Castro (Madrid: Espasa-Calpe, 1958), vol. 1; Tirso de Molina, The Trickster of Seville and the Stone Guest, trans. Gwynne Edwards (Warminster: Aris and Phillips, 1986). Cf. Alfonso de Toro, Von den Ähnlichkeiten und Differenzen: Ehre und Drama des 16. und 17. Jahrhunderts in Italien und Spanien (Frankfurt: Vervuert, 1993). See also José-Manuel Losada-Goya, L'honneur au théâtre: La conception de l'honneur dans le théâtre espagnol et français du XVIIᵉ siècle (Paris: Klincksieck, 1994).

2. Tirso de Molina, El burlador de Sevilla, act 2, lines 270–73; Tirso de Molina, The Trickster of Seville, act 2, lines 270–73.

3. René Schérer, *Zeus hospitalier: Eloge de l'hospitalité: Essai philosophique* (Paris: A. Colin, 1993).

4. Joachim Latacz, *Homer: Der erste Dichter des Abendlands* (Munich: Artemis, 1989), 182.

5. See Norbert Elias, *The Civilizing Process: Sociogenetic and Psychogenetic Investigations*, trans. Edmund Jephcott (Oxford: Blackwell, 1994). On contemporary forms of politeness, see Michel Lacroix, *De la politesse: Essai sur la littérature du savoir-vivre* (Paris: Julliard, 1990).

6. More detail in Harald Weinrich, "Die fast vergessene Ehre," in *Literatur für Leser: Essays und Aufsätze zur Literaturwissenschaft* (Stuttgart: Kohlhammer, 1971), 164–80.

7. I follow here Johann Wolfgang Goethe, *Faust*, 2 vols., ed. Albrecht Schöne (Frankfurt: Deutscher Klassiker Verlag, 1994).

8. Johann Wolfgang Goethe, *Faust: Part One*, trans. David Luke (Oxford: Oxford University Press, 1987), lines 2611–12.

9. Ibid., lines 2605–8.

10. Johann Wolfgang Goethe, *Conversations with Eckermann*, trans. John Oxenford (San Francisco: North Point, 1984), 172–74.

11. [Anne-Louise-Germaine] Madame de Staël, *Germany*, 2 vols. (New York: Houghton Mifflin, 1859), vol. 1, 362. See also the chapter "Of the Manners and Characters of the Germans," ibid., 30–42: in Germany "the spirit of society exerts but little power" (31), "the lower classes are sufficiently coarse in their manner of proceeding" (35), and "civilization and nature seem not yet to be sufficiently amalgamated together" (37).

12. Goethe, *Faust*, lines 3173–74.

13. Ibid., lines 3166–68.

14. Giovanni Della Casa, *Galateo*, ed. Giorgio Manganelli and Claudio Milanini (Milan: Rizzoli, 1977); Giovanni Della Casa, *Galateo: A Renaissance Treatise on Manners*, trans. Konrad Eisenbichler and Kenneth R. Bartlett (Toronto: Centre for Reformation and Renaissance Studies, 1994).

15. In the words of Giorgio Manganelli, coeditor of the 1977 Italian edition (see n. 14).

16. Giovanni Della Casa, *Galateo: A Renaissance Treatise on Manners*, 37–38.

17. Immanuel Kant, *The Metaphysical Elements of Justice: Part I of The Metaphysics of Morals*, trans. John Ladd (New York: Bobbs-Merrill, 1965), 81; Theodor W. Adorno, *Minima Moralia: Reflections from Damaged Life*, trans. E.F.N. Jephcott (London: Verso, 1978).

18. Baldesar Castiglione, *The Book of the Courtier*, trans. Charles S. Singleton (Garden City, New York: Doubleday, 1959), 1–3.

19. Claude Chauchadis, "La 'loi du duel' et le savoir-vivre de l'homme d'honneur en Espagne au XVIIe siècle," *Savoir-vivre* 1 (1990), 41–62.

20. Alain Montandon and Christiane Montandon-Binet, *Savoir mourir* (Paris: L'Harmattan, 1993).

21. See especially Baltasar Gracián y Morales, *The Oracle: A Manual of the Art of Discretion*, trans. L. B. Walton (London: Dent, 1962). Arthur Schopenhauer translated Gracián's "hand oracle" into German as *Handorakel und Kunst der Weltklugheit*. See also Werner Krauss, "Gracián: Leben und Werk," in *Die Innenseite der Weltgeschichte: Ausgewählte Essays über Sprache und Literatur* (Leipzig: Reclam, 1983), 57–82.

22. Desiderius Erasmus, *The Ciuilitie of Childhode: With the Discipline and Instruction of Children, Distributed in Small and Compe[n]-dious Chapters*, trans. Thomas Paynell (London: John Tisdale, 1560).

23. Alain, "De la politesse" and "De la danse et de la parure," *Système des beaux-arts*, in *Les arts et les dieux*, ed. Georges Bénézé (Paris: Gallimard, 1958), 245, 264–66.

24. [*Takt*: the German word has the second meaning of musical beat.—Trans.]

25. The cited phrase is the title of chap. 4 of Arthur Schopenhauer's *Aphorismen zur Lebensweisheit*. [In the English translation this appears, extended and transformed, as "Position, or a Man's Place in the Estimation of Others"; see Arthur Schopenhauer, *The Wisdom of Life*, trans. T. Bailey Saunders (London: Swan Sonnenschein, 1891), 59–135.—Trans.]

26. On the antagonism of politeness and sincerity, see the preface to Jean-Michel Besnier et al., eds., *Politesse et sincérité* (Paris: Esprit, 1994). [Harald Weinrich's preface appears later in this volume as "Politeness and Sincerity."—Trans.]

27. Alexis de Tocqueville, *Democracy in America*, 2 vols., ed. J. P. Mayer and Max Lerner, trans. George Lawrence (New York: Harper and Row, 1966), vol. 1, 592–602.

28. [Anne-Louise-Germaine] Madame de Staël, *An Extraordinary Woman: Selected Writings of Germaine de Staël*, trans. Vivian Folkenflik (New York: Columbia University Press, 1987), 188–200.

29. Ibid., 188.

30. Ibid., 191.

31. Ibid., 189.

32. Ibid., 200.

33. The distinction between negative and positive polite-

ness has been disseminated above all by Erving Goffman in recent scholarship, following an idea of Durkheim's; see Erving Goffman, *Interaction Ritual: Essays on Face-to-Face Behavior* (New York: Pantheon, 1982). See also Harald Weinrich, *Lügt man im Deutschen, wenn man höflich ist?* (Mannheim: Bibliographisches Institut, 1986), esp. 9.

34. See Pierre Magnard, ed., *La dignité de l'homme: Actes du colloque tenu à la Sorbonne–Paris IV en novembre 1992* (Paris: Champion, 1994).

35. Walter Benjamin, "Ibizan Sequence," in *Selected Writings* (1927–1934), ed. Michael W. Jennings et al., trans. Rodney Livingstone et al. (Cambridge: Belknap Press of Harvard University Press, 1999), vol. 2, 587.

Politeness and Sincerity

Whereas before Kant morality was still expressed in terms of virtues (and immorality in terms of vices), Giovanni Della Casa, the Italian author of a conduct manual titled *Galateo* (1558), translated into French under the title *Galatée* (1562), had already speculated about the moral status of politeness. Is it proper to count politeness among the classical (theological, cardinal) virtues, and can one brave the authority of Aristotle and Saint Thomas so as to open the canonical catalogue to a new category of virtues that we might today call sociable or even social? The author hesitates to go so far and contents himself modestly—I might even say politely—with reclaiming for politeness a moral status close to that of the ethics in force in his time. It may be, he writes, that "sweetness of manners and decorum of demeanor and of speech" are too "frivolous" to be admitted to the coterie of such noble virtues as prudence, justice, courage, and temperance. Compared to these, fine manners are perhaps no more than virtues of appearance. Nevertheless, Della Casa continues, the officially recognized virtues, whatever their importance, are there to be exercised only on grand but rare occasions, whereas a minor virtue like politeness is needed many times daily ("ogni dí molte volte"). Also, failures in this minor virtue, by their very frequency, can easily irritate and annoy the company more than is justified by the facts themselves. "Men fear wild beasts but have no fear of smaller animals such as mosquitoes or flies; still, because these insects are constant pests, men complain more often about them than about wild beasts."[1]

Our author's desire to bring great and small morals together does not end there. In the next chapter of his treatise he offers a strikingly laconic definition of politeness in a remarkable maxim: "It will be to your advantage to temper and adapt your manners not according to your own choices but according to the pleasure of those with whom you are dealing and act accordingly" ("Conviensi fare dell'altrui voglia suo piacere").[2] In what moral treatise can one find a greater homage to the values of altruism than in this maxim of a so-called minor morality! Still, the author warns us against two intrinsic obstacles to this praiseworthy altruistic politeness: "When someone delights too much in favouring someone else's wishes in conversation or in behavior he appears to be more of a buffoon or a jester, or perhaps a flatterer, rather than a well-mannered gentleman. And, on the contrary, someone who does not give a thought to another's pleasure or displeasure is boorish, unmannered, and unattractive."[3] It is thus by the two extremes, that of the "too much" and that of the "too little," that one can sin against the rules of politeness, which occupies the middle ground between these two poles. This is the classical position of *mesótès* or *aurea mediocritas*, such as Aristotle assigned to virtue in his *Nicomachean Ethics*. The two scoundrels flanking virtue here are the best proof that politeness has acquired the status of a virtue—a minor one, to be sure, but still unquestionably authentic.

All in all, European society succeeded very well, in a long process of "civilization,"[4] in chasing the flies of impoliteness and the mosquitoes of incivility—better than it succeeded, alas, in banishing the beasts and monsters of immorality and crime from the world. Indeed, in the seventeenth and eighteenth centuries a culture of politeness bloomed and flourished throughout Europe with a splendor that in many respects eclipsed the often cloudy varnish of the ancient virtues. Soon France—the court as well as the city—passed in the eyes of Europe for "the center of good taste and politeness" (La Bruyère). In France more than elsewhere, and in particular in the honesty of the *honnête homme*, the politeness of manners was strictly conflated with moral virtue, which led Joseph Joubert, the moralist of the Enlightenment, to affirm: "He who is insufficiently polite is not human."

Then came the moment when, full of the triumph of the new universal virtue, a character in Marivaux, mistress of a salon where polite conversation is cultivated like a liturgy, wearies of these eternal sweets and finally discovers, disillusioned and losing heart, that "the whole earth is polite." The heroine of this comedy, *Les Sincères* (1739), languishes for the unheard-of charms of a distant and unexplored country whose name is: sincerity. Unfortunately, she still aspires at once to two desires that are hardly compatible: to live in total sincerity and to be recognized as the most beautiful of women. And so this marquise is laughed at, as was, in the previous century, Alceste, constrained to practice his misanthropic sincerity away from the "world," in the solitude of a desert.

Such was not proper pleasure, according to Rousseau, citizen of Geneva. For him, French politeness as it was cultivated with such refinement in Parisian salons was all artifice and affectation and served only to display "the appearances of all the virtues without having a single one." This politeness, certainly of manners and perhaps of mind, was in no way comparable to a politeness of the heart such as might be supposed in natural man and should be advocated in Emile's education. He would certainly not be judged polite by the conventions of good society, but he will be sincere. Once "this uniform and perfidious veil of politeness" is gone, the truth of virtue will appear, and the world will know: "It suffices to be good." Next to this universal virtue, all the little virtues or appearances of virtue that can be found in the artificial behavior of the polite are no better than brilliant dust.

We, men and women living more than two centuries later, have all become citizens of Geneva, to the point of valuing the most authentic sincerity above any other quality, however many flies and mosquitoes may be drawn to this shining light in our modern moral code. It hardly costs us anything, therefore, to cry out in the town square (and this with no question mark): "Politeness is dead, long live Sincerity!" But is it truly dead, this politeness of yesteryear, and—perhaps a more urgent question yet—is this virtue of sincerity truly alive enough to merit the praise and flattery of its numerous contemporary courtiers?

It is here that we should place a large question mark.

NOTES

1. Giovanni Della Casa, *Galateo: A Renaissance Treatise on Manners*, trans. Konrad Eisenbichler and Kenneth R. Bartlett (Toronto: Centre for Reformation and Renaissance Studies, 1994), 32–33.

2. Ibid., 33.

3. Ibid.

4. Norbert Elias, *The Civilizing Process: Sociogenetic and Psychogenetic Investigations*, trans. Edmund Jephcott (Oxford: Blackwell, 1994).

The Style Is the Man Is the Devil

The title of this essay combines two quotations from French literature. The first comes from the Comte de Buffon and has become proverbial outside France as well. In its usual form it reads: *Le style c'est l'homme* (The style is the man). The second quotation is from Valéry and alludes to Buffon: *Le style c'est le diable* (Style is the devil). Actually, however, it is not Paul Valéry but the devil himself who says this, in Valéry's Faust play, *Mon Faust* (1946). Since the old rule probably still holds, speak but of the devil and he will appear, I shall begin, as a precaution to exorcise him, in reverse chronological order with Valéry's devil. Then, afterward, the focus will shift to Buffon's "man." In a third and last section there will follow some conclusions about the situation of stylistics today.

Paul Valéry (1871–1945) wrote his fragmentary Faust drama during the war and the German occupation. Unlike Thomas Mann's novel *Doctor Faustus* (1947), however, it did not turn into a critical analysis of Germany's "demonic" history but rather into a critical reflection on the glory and misery of the creative spirit in the modern world, in accord with Valéry's dominant thematics. In such a work the devil also has his place. He is called Mephistopheles, as in Goethe, and also resembles Goethe's figure in many qualities of his devilishly civilized character. The other protagonist of the play—though no more than Mephistopheles—is Faust himself, who is also shaped on Goethe's model but differs from it in some aspects of his scientific modernity. According to Valéry, he should remind the reader of Einstein or Heisenberg. He is further distinguished from Goethe's Faust in that he is a passionate writer or at least aspires to be one. To be sure, we do see Goethe's Faust with pen in hand. He labors mightily at translating the opening of the Book of John into his beloved German. But this attempt at authorship is interrupted at once, right after he finds a good translation of the first verse.

In this respect, Valéry's Faust is a writer of an entirely different caliber. He is full of the ambition to write a unique and unheard-of book that will simultaneously be a scholarly and literary work of total and universal significance and will summarize all other works of world literature and thereby render them superfluous. It can therefore be called simply "the Book" (le Livre). Faust makes his pact with the devil precisely so that he can write this definitive book:

Faust
Very well, let us make a pact. . . .

Mephisto
You haven't said anything yet.

Faust
Listen: I want to create a great work, a book. . . .

Mephisto
You? Aren't you satisfied with *being* a book?

Faust
I have special reasons for this one. I want it to be an inextricable blend of my true and my false memories, my ideas, my intuitions, my well-conducted hypotheses and deductions, my experiments with the imagination: all my diverse voices in one! A book one could begin at any point and leave off at any other. . . .

Mephisto
That's nothing new. Every reader sees to that.

Faust
Perhaps no one will read it; but anyone who does will never be able to read another.

In his succeeding replies in this dialogue with the devil, Faust describes the style of this book as follows:

Faust
I want this book to be written in a style of my own invention, a style that will glide with marvelous ease from the bizarre to the commonplace and back again, from absolute fantasy

to the most rational rigor, from prose to verse, from the
veriest platitude to the most fragile of . . . ideals.

Mephistopheles drily interrupts Faust's torrent of words
and replies mockingly:

Mephisto
Ho, ho, ho! . . . It's easy to see we are old friends. Your
ideal style seems to me altogether Mephistophelean,
Mr. Author. Style, in fact, is . . . the Devil.[1]

With this reply, Mephistopheles reveals his superb knowledge of literature. It is not only that he evidently knows
Buffon, whose quotation he distorts. He also knows that
the Book has existed for a long time, indeed in two com-
peting versions. The first is the Book of Books, as Christians
call it, the Bible. This book, inspired by the Holy Ghost,
stands above all other books and, for pious souls, has not
infrequently replaced them. The second version is the lay
variant of the first. Stéphane Mallarmé (1842–1898) was
obsessed with this idea and conceived of his entire literary production as preparation for a unique and definitive
book, which he also wanted to call, simply and immod-
estly, the Book (le Livre).[2] Mallarmé scholars disagree as
to whether he ever actually wrote any of this book, at least
in fragmentary form. If not, then we shall perhaps have to
get the librarians of Jorge Luis Borges's "Library of Babel"
(1941) to seek further for this unheard-of book.[3]

Mephistopheles in any case grasped exactly what lurks
behind Faust's plan for a book: the sins of pride and

hubris, in which as devil he is an expert: *Eritis sicut Deus.* . . .
So let us be warned away from this temptation by Valéry's
dialogue between Faust and Mephistopheles and bring our
claims for style down to a more human level. Can Buffon
assist us here?

Georges Louis Leclerc, Comte de Buffon (1707–1788),
is known in literature for two quite disparate achievements. The one, extremely short, is his dictum *Le style c'est
l'homme*; the other, extremely long, is his forty-four-volume
natural history, which appeared—in part posthumously—
from 1749 to 1804 under the impressive title *Natural History,
General and Particular*.[4] This work was extremely successful
in its time. Its author was praised as a "new Aristotle" or
a "French Pliny." Wolf Lepenies, who has written in detail
on the European reception of Buffon, cites one admirer,
who wrote the following verses in Buffon's honor:

> O jour le plus beau de ma vie!
> J'ai satisfait ma noble envie,
> J'ai vu Buffon. . . . Je suis content!
>
> O greatest day of my life!
> My highest wish is satisfied,
> I've seen Buffon. . . . Now I am happy![5]

The remarkable success achieved among readers and critics by Buffon's natural history, from its first volume, is to
be ascribed chiefly to the style in which the work is written. There soon appeared the admiring expression *style
Buffon*. His style consists primarily in the fact that Buffon

carried over into his natural history the traditional doctrine of the three literary styles, which are famously associated with the three ranks of society. Just as aristocracy, bourgeoisie, and peasantry were distinguished in society, and each had its appropriate assigned style—*stilus sublimis, stilus mediocris,* or *stilus humilis*—so in Buffon the natural types were analogously to be distinguished by rank, and a similar hierarchy of styles was required to describe them.[6]

In Buffon's hierarchy, for example, *lion, horse,* and *swan* were animal kinds that required a "sublime" descriptive language on the model of the human ranks *king, knight,* and *poet.* And so the swan is described in the natural history:

> The graces of figure, the beauty of shape, correspond in the Swan to the mildness of his disposition: he pleases every eye; he decorates and embellishes every place that he frequents; he is beloved, extolled, admired; and no species more deserves our applause. On none has Nature ever diffused so much of those noble and gentle graces, which recal the image of her most charming productions: elegant fashion of body; roundness of form; softness of outline; whiteness resplendent and pure; motions full of flexibility and expression; attitudes, sometimes animated, sometimes gently languishing. All the features and actions of the Swan breathe the voluptuousness, the enchantment which wrap our soul at the sight of grace and beauty; all declare it, paint it, the bird of love; all justify the ingen-

ious and sprightly mythology, that this delightful bird was
the father of the most beautiful of women.[7]

Buffon's sublime style rises to such ethereal heights whenever the object seems to require such a song of songs. This
brings us, of course, back to the vicinity of Goethe's
Mephistopheles, who also rests his hopes of winning his
bet with Faust on the irresistible charms of beautiful
Helen. But we must again emphasize that Buffon by no
means always frequents such heights. To be sure, he
counts the grand orderliness of Nature among the elevated
objects that require sublime style, but mice and rats, by
contrast, get low style, and by and large the middle style
predominates in his work.

But posterity did not judge him in so nuanced a fashion, for however unreservedly his first readers and critics
admired him, a second generation of critics soon savaged
him (but not his numerous readers, who remained loyal
to him much longer) as a chatterer and windbag who
brought science into discredit with his style: "a peacock
showing off his feathers," in the words of a contemporary,
the moralist Joseph Joubert.[8] Particularly dangerous hos-
tility developed against him among the followers of Carl
von Linné. The Swedish naturalist had already published
a first version of his *Systema Naturae* in 1735, before Buffon,
and had thereby demonstrated how a comprehensive
description of nature entirely without style, in the form of
a dry Latin nomenclature, can succeed in science so long
as it is strictly methodical. For *swan*, for example, there is

only the dry distinction between *cygnus ferus* and *cygnus mansuetus*.[9] And soon the Linnaeans looked down with scorn on Buffon from the heights of their exact taxonomy and attacked him with the dangerous phrase "Stylo primus, doctrina ultimus." The label stuck. Buffon's reputation never recovered from this criticism, and since then he has had no place in the history of the exact sciences.

But the devil still has a few surprises in store for us regarding Buffon. At the height of his literary fame, in 1753, just a few years after the first volume of his natural history had appeared, Buffon was elected to the Académie Française. Since he had already been inducted for his scientific achievement into the Paris Academy of Sciences— in the section for mechanics, by the way—we may take his induction into the Académie Française, the institution specifically for language, as homage to the writer and as acknowledgment of his literary style. This is strikingly confirmed by the fact that Buffon gave his inaugural lecture (his *discours de réception*) before the forty immortals of this august body on the topic of style, so that this speech is often titled "Discourse on Style."[10] In this discourse we find what Heinrich Laube called "that beautiful sentence" that has made Buffon better known throughout the world than his forty-four volumes of natural history, "Le style c'est l'homme," on which Laube remarked in 1835, "Anyone who talks about style has to be familiar with Buffon."[11]

Is this sentence now as truly remarkable as one would conclude from its overwhelming reception? Actually, Buffon didn't say anything new. As Wolfgang G. Müller has demonstrated in detail, it has been a "topos" since antiquity that the manner in which someone speaks or writes reveals his essence and character.[12] We find in Cicero, for example, "Qualis autem homo ipse esset, talem esse eius orationem" ("Whatever the nature of the man himself, such is his style of speech").[13] And even in Buffon, the sentence stands in a rather inconspicuous part of this discourse. Now, it is essential to know that the strict stylistic conventions of the Académie Française require three parts for the inaugural lecture of a new member: first, praise of the academy and of the deceased predecessor whose chair is being filled; then a somewhat freer thematic section; and, finally, a third, closing part, in which the academy is to be addressed again and its members thanked. The sentence in question is in this last section, and not in the thematic section. An apostrophe to the members present ("Gentlemen") precedes it, in addition to praise of their "sublime" works, combined with a public acknowledgment of the stimulation he has received from reading them. There then follows in Buffon another specific reflection on how actually to achieve that "immortality" which the forty members of the Académie Française so notoriously possess. This question is of particular relevance for someone who, like Buffon, is not actually a writer but a scientist. For this reason, Buffon confesses specifically that, to his mind, scientific achievements ("knowledge, facts, and discoveries")[14] do not alone suffice for immortality. The scientist still must have an exquisite style, and indeed one that is "elevated, noble, sublime,"[15] to make his scientific work worthy of immortality; for here the maxim applies that "the well-written works are the only ones that will go down to posterity." In my opinion, that is actually the most interesting if also the most disputable statement in Buffon's speech. The more famous dictum, which pales in comparison, reads in its original version: "Le style est l'homme même" (The style is the man himself).

Evidently the devil had a finger in the pie here. Buffon's dictum is almost never cited as it actually reads in the text. The quasi-Mephistophelian humor in the situation is pointed out with a wink by the French stylist Pierre Guiraud in a paradoxical formulation that reads: "Whatever Buffon may have to say about it: the style is the man."[16] Is the distinction thus ironically emphasized important or not? To answer this question, we must examine the immediate context of the dictum somewhat more closely. It reads:

> The well-written works are the only ones that will go down to posterity: the amount of knowledge in a book, the peculiarity of the facts, the novelty even of the discoveries, are not sure warrants of immortality. If the works that contain these are concerned with only minor objects; if they are written without taste, without nobility, without inspiration, they will perish; since the knowledge, facts, and discoveries, being easily detached, are passed on to others, and even gain intrinsically when appropriated by more gifted hands. These things are external to the man; the style is the man himself.[17]

We learn from the context: what a person is *himself*, his style, is inside him, in contrast to the broad factual knowledge that is his business as a scientist and that, despite its obvious value, remains external to him and, to that extent, always at risk on the path to immortality. Behind the statement lurks an old distinction, well known and much discussed since antiquity, between *res* and *verba* (*choses* and *mots*, things and words). In the ideal case, as Buffon clearly believes is his own, these work together, since he is simultaneously a member of the academy of science, for his *res/choses*, and of the academy of language, for his *verba/mots*. That is the very pragmatic sense of the sentence in question—to position the chair of the new member within the Académie Française.

In order for a world-famous dictum with a completely different meaning—or several different meanings—to develop, the sentence had to change, first of all formally. For use in textual isolation, it had to get rid of its contrastive *même* (-self), which makes no sense without the preceding context. For the same purpose, it was also useful though not absolutely necessary to rhematize the predicate noun *l'homme* with the presentative morpheme *c'est*, which focuses the meaning to a semantic position between the English expressions "The style is the man" and "Style makes the man."[18]

As far as meaning is concerned, the dictum's separation from the context of Buffon's discourse to the academy brings about a push and a pull that are both caused by history. The push originates in the past, that is, in the version of the topic already formulated by Cicero, which validates Buffon's dictum as a classical maxim. But there is an equally powerful pull from the future, namely, from pre-Romanticism and Romanticism, which, as they increasingly penetrated public consciousness after Buffon's death, lent a new anthropological dignity to the unique individual and his experience. Thus Buffon's dictum, now promoted to the status of a general maxim, was able to become a slogan for a stylistics of the individual—something Buffon the scientist and society man would never have dreamed of. If the devil did not have a hand in this dreadfully tangled reception, I have no idea how else such a concatenation of contingencies might be explained.

I would now like to derive from these historical observations on Buffon and Valéry a few conclusions that apply to stylistics at the present time:

1. This examination of Buffon and Valéry, who both considered themselves scholars, though in quite different senses, shows that there is still no coherent stylistics of scholarly literature, despite the worthy efforts of the linguists and literary scholars, among students of style. We have, to be sure, a well-established functional stylistics and, related to it methodologically, a blossoming stylistics of disciplinary discourses, but the vast body of scholarly and pedagogical writing in all disciplines has as yet scarcely been described and analyzed in stylistic terms. Evidently we have been intimidated by the prestige of scientific "objectivity,"

according to which "the object itself" and nothing else finds expression in the sciences, insofar as they can lay claim to precision; and so we students of stylistics have largely turned away from this scholarly literature and left it to itself. Usually we are content if the editors of the most important scholarly journals provide their authors with style sheets, which guarantee a certain formal uniformity to the publications. I would therefore call emphatically for a stylistics of scholarly literature, which would also extend to the forms of oral communication in the sciences. Such a stylistics cannot be derived from the stylistics of belles lettres and must also be distinguished clearly from a (functional) stylistics of journalism and the other media of public communication.

2. Furthermore, the example of Buffon as author shows that it is risky and dangerous to try to serve two masters at once. Buffon tried to borrow stylistic glamour from belles lettres for the forty-four volumes of his scientific work. That made it easy for the devil to raise him high at first, so that his fall would be all the harder. "Stylo primus, doctrina ultimus" is an infernal criticism, and there is surely a pinch of devilish irony in the fact that this author of forty-four volumes was immortalized not by this enormous exertion but by a short and multiply misunderstood sentence on the margins of his scholarly work. As a counterexample, I will mention the man who was keeper of the Royal Garden in Berlin for Prussia, essentially the same office that Buffon had held a century earlier in Paris. This was Adelbert von Chamisso, who kept his literary work (in German)—a lot

of good poetry and an immortal tale, "Peter Schlemihl"—
strictly separated from his twice as voluminous botanical
and zoological works, written mostly in Latin and French.
As a result, he could be acknowledged by Thomas Mann
as a classic German poet, on the one hand, and, on the
other, by Charles Darwin as a "highly distinguished naturalist." This is an author who also understood the devil
thoroughly and discovered, in the guise of the "gray
figure" to whom Peter Schlemihl consigns his soul, the
unobtrusiveness of the modern devil.[19]

3. We shall concentrate for the moment only on the figure
of Faust in Valéry and take this scholar, even more than
Goethe's Faust, as a warning that the trees of stylistics do
not grow all the way to heaven. Grandeur of manner, sub-
limity of style are possible only under certain conditions,
which also set limits to stylistic grandeur. The Faustian
striving for an absolute style, realized in a definitive book
that will make all other books forgotten: this extravagant
project is hardly new to the devil and is called pride or hubris.
The temptation is even more dangerous for the language
of science than for that of poetry. For the first maxim of a
stylistics of scholarly writing would surely have to read: "In
the sciences, only *contributions* to knowledge are possible;
therefore, it is necessary to write so that one's predeces-
sors can be identified and one's successors imagined."

4. Everyone knows that the devil is in the details. With regard
to stylistics, this means that a quasi-Mephistophelian
temptation lurks not only in extravagantly ambitious style
but also in immeasurably low style. In the effort to bring

literary style down from the sublime heights on which, as we have seen, it can lose its way, linguistic stylistics has occasionally, not without a triumphant flourish, spread the word that style is an ordinary, mundane affair. Everything, but everything, has style. This banal assertion doubtless affords the devil great joy—if not Goethe's or Valéry's devil, then perhaps Chamisso's gray one. For there are no consequences in exchanging the sentence "Everything has style" for "Nothing has style." To the devil with literary stylistics! Is that really what we want?

5. When Buffon decided at age forty-two to write his great natural history, scientific knowledge could still be surveyed more or less comprehensively, and the author had reason to hope he might summarize everything relevant about our planet and its conditions of life in a single work in a finite span of time. This plan did not succeed. There is not a single research center for geology or zoology today where anyone would turn to this work in order to orient himself in the field. And yet these volumes can be purchased secondhand, inexpensively and in beautiful bindings, in French bookstores. But who has space in his library for forty-four volumes of Buffon? All private libraries and even public ones are already bursting. This brings us back to Valéry, in whose work the constant overproduction of books and the limitless reproduction and circulation of other forms of information constitute the central motivation for his Doctor Faust's attempt to swim against the stream and reduce the masses of data to a single book. Even if this idea is doomed to failure, I would still like to conclude from

the attempt (and from the temptation!) that a stylistics of scholarly literature under today's conditions of communication would seriously have to raise the question of how any single scholar can make his contribution noticeable at all in this universal noise. Perhaps Buffon was right, after all, with his maxim, two hundred fifty years ago, that only through style does one survive for posterity. With this maxim in mind, he developed his *style Buffon* and thereby promptly failed to survive. Hence I will not subscribe to it and will instead draw the negative conclusion prompted by his case, that a bad stylistic decision can cause even a scientist to miss out on posterity.

6. The question of a correct stylistic decision for the circumstances remains unanswered. I am convinced, however, that even in scholarly communication, just as in poetic and literary communication, authors still have the need to be recognized as individuals who make a contribution. We must not let ourselves be deceived by the existence of high-capacity electronic facilities for storing the scientific results accumulating in masses, in which all data must necessarily be deindividualized and stylistically leveled. They may be indispensable for the functioning of what Thomas S. Kuhn called "normal science," but a line from *Kiosk*, Hans Magnus Enzensberger's collection of poems, probably also applies: "stored, i.e. forgotten."[20] A stylistics of scholarly literature would thus have to ask after the circumstances under which scientific memory *really* functions and the significance of style in that case, as the condition of social visibility and noticeability. To my

mind, the question of the relation between style and memory, raised for the first time by Susan Sontag in her essay "On Style" (1965), deserves special attention for the future of stylistics altogether, in the scientific and in, if I may call it that, the literary literature.[21]

7. Even though I have insisted that the stylistics of scholarly literature be developed independently of the current stylistics of literature in the narrower sense, the two nevertheless really should stimulate one another. For example, the basically incorrect assertion of many scientists, that they manage without any style at all and that they let "the object itself" speak, could perhaps encourage us to pay more attention to privative qualities in poetic and literary stylistics and to evaluate them stylistically. Under the current conditions of mass production and overproduction in this sphere also—one has only to visit a book fair—it becomes ever less probable that an author can draw attention to his work simply by using *more* metaphors, *more* metonymies, *more* oxymorons, or *more* ornamental modifiers. Works are noticed these days more often for understated than for overstated use of language, more for a negative than for a positive stylistics. But whether this law of privation holds for all circumstances and occasions must remain an open question.

NOTES

1. Paul Valéry, *My Faust*, in *Plays*, trans. David Paul and Robert Fitzgerald (New York: Pantheon, 1960), 32–33 (Valéry's ellipses). On the interpretation of this drama, see Karl-Alfred Blüher,

Strategie des Geistes: Paul Valérys 'Faust' (Frankfurt: Klostermann, 1960); Karl-Alfred Blüher and Jürgen Schmidt-Radefeldt, eds., Paul Valéry: Le cycle de 'Mon Faust' devant la sémiotique théâtrale et l'analyse textuelle: Colloque international de Kiel, 15–17 octobre 1977 (Tübingen: Narr, 1991); Victor Hell, "'Le style, c'est le diable' (P. Valéry, 'Mon Faust'): Création et satanisme dans 'Mon Faust' de Valéry et dans le 'Dr. Faustus' de Thomas Mann," in Monique Parent Frazee and Jean Levaillant, eds., Paul Valéry Contemporain (Paris: Klincksieck, 1974), 194–208.

2. Everything important about the idea of "the" book can be found in Stéphane Mallarmé and Jacques Scherer, Le "Livre" de Mallarmé: Premières recherches sur des documents inédits (Paris: Gallimard, 1957). See also Paul Bénichou, Selon Mallarmé (Paris: Gallimard, 1995).

3. Jorge Luis Borges, "The Library of Babel," trans. Anthony Kerrigan, in Ficciones (New York: Grove, 1962), 79–88. See also Heinz Schlaffer, Borges (Frankfurt: Fischer, 1993).

4. [Georges Louis Leclerc], Comte de Buffon, Natural History, General and Particular, 20 vols., trans. William Smellie (London: T. Cadell and W. Davies, 1812). For scholarship on Buffon, see Jean-Claude Beaune and Jean Gayon, Buffon 88: Actes du colloque international pour le bicentenaire de la mort de Buffon (Paris: Vrin, 1992).

5. Wolf Lepenies, Das Ende der Naturgeschichte (Munich: Hanser, 1976), esp. 142–47. See also Wolf Lepenies, Autoren und Wissenschaftler im 18. Jahrhundert: Linné, Buffon, Winckelmann, Georg Forster, Erasmus Darwin (Munich: Hanser, 1988), esp. 63.

6. The clearest description of the doctrine of the three styles is to be found in Erich Auerbach, Mimesis: The Representation of

Reality in Western Literature, trans. Willard R. Trask (Princeton: Princeton University Press, 1953).

7. Buffon, *Natural History*, vol. 19, 491–92.

8. Joseph Joubert, *Carnets*, ed. André Beaunier and André Bellessort (Paris: Gallimard, 1938), 200.

9. Carl von Linné, *Systema naturae per regna tria naturae, secundum classes, ordines, genera, species, cum characteribus, differentiis, synonymis, locis* (Stockholm: L. Salvii, 1766–68), 194.

10. [Georges Louis Leclerc], Comte de Buffon, "Discourse on Style," in *Theories of Style*, ed. Lane Cooper (New York: Macmillan, 1909), 169–79.

11. Heinrich Laube, *Moderne Charakteristiken*, 2 vols. (Mannheim: C. Löwenthal, 1835), vol. 2, 232.

12. Wolfgang G. Müller, "Das Diktum 'Le style est l'homme même,'" in *Topik des Stilbegriffs: Zur Geschichte des Stilverständnisses von der Antike bis zur Gegenwart* (Darmstadt: Wissenschaftliche Buchgesellschaft, 1981), 40–51.

13. Cited in Müller, *Topik des Stilbegriffs*, 12. See also Cicero, *Tusculan Disputations II and V. With a Summary of III and IV*, 5.47, ed. and trans. A. E. Douglas (Warminster: Aris and Phillips, 1990), 106, 107.

14. Pierre Guiraud, *La stylistique* (Paris: Presses Universitaires de France, 1954), 177.

15. Ibid., 178.

16. On Buffon's dictum, see (besides Müller, "Das Diktum") Michel Espagne, "'Le style est l'homme même': A priori esthétique et écriture scientifique chez Buffon et Winckelmann," in Almuth Grésillon and Michaël Werner, eds., *Leçon d'écriture, ce que*

disent les manuscrits (Paris: Lettres modernes, 1985), 51–67; Jürgen Trabant, "'Le style est l'homme même': Quel homme?" *Comparatio* 2–3 (1991), 52–72; Hans Martin Gauger, "Graf Buffon über den Stil oder 'Stil ist der Mensch selbst,'" in *Über Sprache und Stil* (Munich: Beck, 1995), 203–7.

17. Guiraud, *Le stylistique*, 177–78. See also Gauger, *Über Sprache und Stil*, 204.

18. The distinction *res/verba* is central in the mnemotechnics of ancient rhetoric, in the form *memoria rerum* and *memoria verborum*; discussed at greater length in Harald Weinrich, *La mémoire linguistique de l'Europe* (Paris: Collège de France, 1990). Especially important in this context for the eighteenth century is [Jean Le Rond] d'Alembert, "Reflections on Elocution, and Style in General," in *Miscellaneous Pieces* (London, 1764), 29–55, esp. 34.

19. I have discussed Chamisso as poet and scientist at greater length in Harald Weinrich, "Chamissos Gedächtnis," *Der gefundene Schatten: Chamisso-Reden 1985 bis 1993*, ed. Dietrich Krusche (Munich: A1, 1993), 127–46.

20. Thomas S. Kuhn, *The Structure of Scientific Revolutions* (Chicago: University of Chicago Press, 1962); Hans Magnus Enzensberger, "Flight of Ideas (I)," in *Kiosk*, trans. Michael Hamburger (Newcastle upon Tyne: Bloodaxe, 1997), 26.

21. Susan Sontag, "On Style," in *Against Interpretation and Other Essays* (New York: Farrar, Straus and Giroux, 1966), 15–38.

Library of Congress Cataloging-in-Publication Data

Weinrich, Harald.

The linguistics of lying and other essays /

Harald Weinrich; translated and introduced

by Jane K. Brown and Marshall Brown.

p. cm. — (Literary conjugations)

ISBN 0-295-98549-6 (pbk. : alk. paper)

1. Linguistics.

2. Truthfulness and falsehood.

3. Politeness (Linguistics)

I. Title.   II. Series.

P125.W45 2005   410—dc22   2005016955